THE POWER OF THE CROSS

Books by Mahesh and Bonnie Chavda

The Hidden Power of Watching and Praying

40 Days of Prayer and Fasting

The Hidden Power of a Woman

The Hidden Power of Healing Prayer

The Hidden Power of Prayer and Fasting Revised

The Hidden Power of Speaking in Tongues

The Hidden Power of the Blood of Jesus

Original Sin

Threshold of Glory by Dotty Schmitt, Bonnie Chavda, et al.

Available from Destiny Image Publishers

THE POWER OF THE CROSS

EPICENTER OF GLORY

MAHESH
and
BONNIE CHAVDA

DESTINY IMAGE® PUBLISHERS, INC.

P.O. Box 310, Shippensburg, PA 17257-0310

"Speaking to the Purposes of God for This Generation and for the Generations to Come."

This book and all other Destiny Image, Revival Press, MercyPlace, Fresh Bread, Destiny Image Fiction, and Treasure House books are available at Christian bookstores and distributors worldwide.

For a U.S. bookstore nearest you, call 1-800-722-6774.

For more information on foreign distributors, call 717-532-3040.

Reach us on the Internet: www.destinyimage.com.

Trade Paper ISBN 13: 978-0-7684-3246-6

Hardcover ISBN 13: 978-0-7684-3432-3

Large Print ISBN 13: 978-0-7684-3433-0

E-book ISBN 13: 978-0-7684-9123-4

For Worldwide Distribution, Printed in the U.S.A.

3 4 5 6 7 8 9 10 11 / 13 12 11

DEDICATION

This book is dedicated to a champion of the cross, Elena Cruz, one-hundred years old at this writing, who radiates the glorious Presence in the face of us all.

Far be from me to glory except in the cross of our Lord Jesus Christ, by which the world has been crucified to me, and I to the world (Galatians 6:14 ESV).

CONTENTS

FOREWORD

We are living in an age of amazing and increasing revival. It is a time of great supernatural awakening.

Carol and I were surprised and overwhelmed by the Holy Spirit as God poured out the renewal known as the Toronto Blessing almost two decades ago. It has been our privilege to be a part of stewarding a wonderful move of God that has touched the nations with the Father's love and has awakened the Church to step into His glorious presence. Among the people that we have known who have helped steward the ongoing move of the Holy Spirit are Mahesh and Bonnie Chavda. The Chavdas carry a rare gift to interweave anointed biblical teaching with living testimonies from their own life and ministry that impart faith, love, and hunger for more of God.

The Power of the Cross: Epicenter of Glory is born out of real-life encounters with the God of glory day by day. This book is a powerful tool that will inspire, delight, and anoint you to personally experience and participate in one of the most significant eras in the history of the world. God has ordained to make His home inside everyone who receives Him. It is one of the greatest miracles you can experience. In our quest to know more about the move of the Spirit and learning how to steward revival, we learned that the Spirit of God was most at home when we kept Jesus and His cross at the center of what we were experiencing. Mahesh and Bonnie are servants of the Lord who have chosen to embrace the cross and revel in the glory of the Father. *The Power of the Cross: Epicenter of Glory* leads us on a journey *to* the cross and *through* the cross to resurrection glory, and imparts a grace to follow. As the Chavdas say:

> The truth and effectiveness of the cross is simple enough for a child to enter fully. What happened at the cross when God reconciled the world to Himself is a mystery we shall keep discovering for all eternity. Like the cascading force unleashed in the splitting of an atom, the action of Calvary will be ever unfolding in power. The glory of the cross is an explosive, eternal, energy-creating, continually unfolding revelation of beauty. The cross is the glory of God. In it we behold Him as He really is. Calvary must not be an aversion, or a thing of the past. For as long as we have mortal flesh, as long as we seek His power, we will find Him at the cross.
>
> Because the cross is the singular demonstration of the overwhelming mercy of God, it remains the key to experiencing the glory of God. The cross reveals God as He is. It shows Him perfect, self-giving, irresistible, humble, absolutely omnipotent in power—and completely obsessed with His love for us.

We love the presence and miracles of God. During the outpouring in Toronto, the Holy Spirit came and revealed the Father's love; Christ and His cross are the only and supreme doorway to God's love and power outpoured and experienced personally. The cross of Jesus is the epicenter of supernatural encounter, change, healing, and joy. Through the cross to the resurrection of Christ, to Heaven's throne and back again to earth, the Holy Spirit is working. A return to fresh encounter with the reality and centrality of the Christ and His cross is the doorway into the next great move of His Spirit. We invite you to step into the ever-unfolding story of His glory. In anticipation of that, Carol and I are thrilled to recommend this timely book by our good friends, Mahesh and Bonnie, as they direct our hearts to the cross and to the glory.

JOHN AND CAROL ARNOTT

When I (Mahesh) was a poor college student attending Texas Tech, I made my way to Dallas to go to a weeklong seminar. I did not have two pennies to rub together, so I was thrilled when I happened to run into a family I knew from Lubbock in the midst of the huge crowd of people. They were staying at a friend's house and were kind enough to say that I was welcome to join them. I was grateful to have a place to stay and did not mind the idea of sleeping on the floor somewhere for the week.

On the first night I went home with these people. We walked into a beautiful house and a lovely woman met us at the door. My friends introduced me, saying, "This is our friend from Kenya who is studying here in America right now and needs a place to stay for the seminar. Can he sleep on the floor or the couch somewhere?" The lady of the house looked straight at me and said, "No." I gulped. Then she continued, "No, he's not going to sleep on the floor or on the couch, he's going to sleep in our master bedroom, and my husband and I will sleep on the couch." I tried to refuse, saying I was happy to sleep on the couch. She said, "You cannot stay unless you sleep in the master bedroom." So I said, "OK."

She closed the door and left me in her big bedroom. There I stood, staring at the king-sized bed, not like anything I had ever been in. I lay down and went to sleep, overwhelmed by God's provision for me. At about 3:00 A.M., a rushing, terrifying sound woke me up. Once I got oriented (this was during the Vietnam War), I realized that it was bombers taking off from the nearby Carswell Air Force Base in Fort Worth, Texas. They kept taking off, one after another, for about an hour and a half. Everything was reverberating with that sound. The house shook; the walls shook; my bed shook. It was quite some time before I was able to go back to sleep.

In the morning, I got up and went to the kitchen in hopes of finding a cup of coffee before heading to the meeting. When I arrived in the kitchen area, my hostess said, "I fixed breakfast for you."

I said, "Thank you. I did not expect that." I turned around and the entire table was filled with food: chicken fried steak, omelets, fried eggs, bacon, gravy, ham, sausage, all kinds of pastries, jams, jellies, and fruit that I had never seen before.

She said, "This is for you. We have already eaten." I wasn't sure what to think, but I sat down gratefully and ate what I could before going to the seminar for the day. That night, the same thing happened. At 3:00 A.M. I was awakened by the jets taking off, and lay awake under that tremendous roar until it finally stopped and I was able to go back to sleep. In the morning, my hostess again had prepared a tremendous feast. She said, "Yesterday we were out of kiwi fruit, but I have some for you today." I wouldn't have noticed. There was no way for me to eat all the food she had prepared. This continued the third, fourth, and fifth day of the seminar.

On the last night, I again went to bed, but when I was awakened in the middle of the night, I realized that there was someone in the room with me. There were golden beams of light surrounding me. I have never seen such wondrous light. It was like living rainbows and all the galaxies of the universe were with me in that room, interspersed with living, golden beams of light.

In the center, I saw Jesus. He had walked into my room. I was completely surrounded by His light and presence. It took my breath away—I was not sure whether I was dead or alive. If I

16

was alive, I wanted to die because I did not ever want to be away from this absolute joy and ecstasy that I was experiencing. There is nothing in human language to describe the utter joy and delight of His presence. All He is was there: truth was coming toward me, life was coming into me, love was coming...I saw right there that light and love and truth is a person, and His name is Jesus Christ.

Then, in the distance, I started hearing a symphony of musical instruments that I had never heard before. This sound of music started to stir and play and reverberate all around me. I suddenly realized that the sound was the jets taking off. But as those sound waves came into the presence of the glory, each sound wave had to bow to the name of Jesus, and it was transformed into a song and glorious symphony praising the Lamb of God.

Everything in the universe must align itself in harmony with our King, Jesus. When you are in the presence of the Lord, His glory will transform you. It will change you. It will change your definitions. That night a lot of my definitions changed because I realized, *It's all in Jesus!* If you have a revelation of the glory, the death of your earthly body acquires a whole new definition. Absent in the body, present with the Lord. There is nothing like the awesome glory of the Lord.

As morning light began to break around 5:30 A.M., the glory started collecting itself together, and the Lord started walking out of the room. I wanted Him to take me with Him. I didn't want to be anywhere but in His presence. But as the glory was gathering and the Lord was about to go, He turned and smiled and said, "I brought you to this house." His eyes were so tender and full of love and compassion, and yet they conveyed complete victory. He went on, "This woman's husband has asked for a divorce, and she cried out to Me. I have put healing in your mouth for their marriage. As you speak, that word will heal them, and their marriage will be restored. I have put the anointing on you." Then He walked off.

I got ready and went out to the kitchen, and again the table was laid out in a sumptuous feast fit for a king. I said to my hostess, "The Lord visited me last night."

She responded, "I know." Then she said, "Several days ago my husband came to me after fourteen years of marriage and said he had found another woman and he was leaving me. My heart broke, and I went into my closet and cried out to God. I have never cried like that, and I asked God to help me. For the first time in my life, I heard the audible voice of God. He said, "I will send My prophet to your home, and when he comes, treat him like you would treat Me, and he will have healing for your home."

She had been expecting me—that was why she had laid out a feast every morning and had given me her master bedroom. She had prepared a place for the Lord of glory to come and touch her and her household. When the seminar ended, I did not go back to that region for nearly fifteen years. But when I did, I found the couple was still happily married from the day the Lord gave me the word.

POWER FROM THE CROSS

The manifest glory of God's presence brings everything else into congruency. He is the tuning fork, and everything else bends to the force of His singing, picking up His vibration and coming along beside Him. The glory is not an "it," nor is it simply the manifestation of miracles or supernatural power. The glory is the effulgence of God's authority, majesty, victory, and the very essence of *"I Am that I Am"* (Exod. 3:14 KJV). The glory is a demonstration of a Person.

In a singular moment in time, the history of creation and the human race was shaken to the core. That moment is an *epikentron,* the central location, the command center that determines the course of every person and all other events. The English word "epicenter" is derived from this Greek word, *epikentron,* meaning "situated on a center." [1] This moment in the whole of created and uncreated history occurred outside the walls of Jerusalem more than two thousand years ago on earth. It was an event that was witnessed by and testified to by many people. The event itself is not contained in time or space or physical or metaphysical dimensions alone. It affects every elemental dimension for eternity. In that moment something new occurred: an old era ended and a new one began. A new race was created. The shroud of death that had fallen like a closing curtain over humanity and all created things was rent in two and rolled back forever.

It happened as the King of Glory shouted, "It is finished!" The cross is the epicenter of the glory of God and His creatures, of time and eternity, of history made and yet to be discovered.

A METAPHOR OF CALVARY

In Ruthwell, Scotland, Dumfriesshire, there is a small chapel. Inside, there stands an 18-foot-tall stone formed into the shape of a cross and covered with pictorial carvings. The full history of the Ruthwell Cross is shrouded, but its impact has been felt since the seventh century, when missionary monks carried the Good News to the pagan and largely illiterate Anglo-Saxons. "Preaching crosses" such as this one, covered with biblical scenes, helped to transmit and preserve the Gospel message. One difference between the Ruthwell Cross and other "high crosses" of Ireland, Scotland, England, and Wales is that the pictures on this cross are surrounded by runic inscriptions. These inscriptions are verses of an ancient poem called *The Dream of the Rood*. The word *rood* means "gallows," and signifies the Roman instrument of death by torture that we call the cross.

After Scotland became a Protestant nation, the Church of Scotland General Assembly passed an act to demolish all religious monuments installed under Catholic tradition. The Ruthwell

Cross was broken down in 1644, and its crushed pieces were scattered throughout the churchyard to be walked upon and forgotten. More than one hundred and fifty years later, the pastor appointed there began to piece it back together. It took him twenty-four years. By 1818, the preaching cross had been reerected, and in 1887 the Ruthwell Cross was declared a protected monument. It was brought indoors to be put on display. The missing crossbeam had to be replaced by a facsimile, and many of the carvings were badly weather-eroded or deliberately defaced. However, for the most part, the runes inscribed there remain legible to this day.

The lines of this ancient poem are the words of a dreamer who encounters the glory of God when the jewel-bedecked tree upon which Jesus died awakens and begins to speak. The dreamer says:

> Listen! The choicest of visions I wish to tell,
> which came as a dream in middle-night...
> It seemed that I saw a most wondrous tree[2]

As described by the dreamer, the cross of Christ outshines the glory of all the kingdoms of this world. The story of the cross is unending. All imaginable bliss was gained there and is to be handed over as a possession to those who find their place beneath its shadow.

The Book of Proverbs tells us, *"It is the glory of God to conceal a matter, but the glory of kings is to search out a matter"* (Prov. 25:2). The search for significance is at the core of what it means to be human. The experience of being wholly unified as a person—spirit, soul, and body—occurs as we experience the glory of God. We will experience the fullness of our being only as we are unified with Christ in God in the resurrection. But until then, God is working by His Spirit to give us glimpses of coming glory. It is our prayer and intention that as you read this book you will begin to find out for yourself the glory of God as it flows through the glorious mystery of the cross, and that in so doing you might be clothed with the splendid royal robe of adoption as a member of His kingly family. It begins at the epicenter of glory: the cross of Jesus Christ.

ENDNOTES

1. See http://encarta.msn.com/dictionary_1861608798/epicenter .html.

2. From *The Dream of the Rood,* lines 1-4. Translation copyright © 1982, Jonathan A. Glenn. Used by permission. For the complete poem as translated from Old English, see http:// www.lightspill.com/poetry/oe/rood.html.

CHAPTER 1

DANCING IN THE DARK

Listen! The choicest of visions I wish to tell,
which came as a dream in middle-night,
after voice-bearers lay at rest.
It seemed that I saw a most wondrous tree
born aloft, wound round by light,
brightest of beams. All was that beacon
sprinkled with gold. Gems stood
fair at earth's corners; there likewise five
shone on the shoulder-span. All there beheld the Angel of God,
fair through predestiny. Indeed, that was
no wicked one's gallows,
but holy souls beheld it there,
men over earth, and all this great creation.
Wondrous that victory-beam....[1]

† † † † † † † † † † † † †

THE young preacher lay shivering in a dank cell
in the lowest dungeon. Half from weak hunger, half
from sleeplessness, he trembled under his damp outer

garment. The hairy thing, like the famous ancient mantle of the first Elijah, gave little succor now.

Clear the way for the Lord in the wilderness; make smooth in the desert a highway for our God...let the rough ground become a plain— the rugged terrain a broad valley; then the glory of the Lord will be revealed...[2]

The words played over and over again in his mind. Mingled with the words were scenes, his cousin and himself playing near the banks of the river that had become the preacher's pulpit, the river in which he baptized the Lamb. Images of his father, dead now. What would he have said to his son if he could speak to him here? Would he reassure him of the story when in the thick darkness of the holy place with only the burning censer for illumination, the glory of God suddenly appeared and took away Zacharias' questioning voice?

Are you the One? The preacher sent his disciples to ask once again—but John's heart burned within him. He knew. The One before whom he had first leaped like David before the ark while he was in Elisabeth's belly. The melody of the Spirit carried strains of glory in a Voice from beyond the confines of that watery cell and his spirit said, "Amen!"

Above him, could he have heard it, strains of a different melody played. The revelry, a sensual, resplendent table of flesh laid out. Herod, his illicit wife, and their guests were transfixed as Salome whirled before the audience. Herodias' request fell in sharp blades upon the king's ear.

John turned his mind back to the river bank. Suddenly, he seemed transported to another era. Elijah stood in the distance surrounded by what began as a cloud of dust. As it rose, the cyclone began to gleam until its brightness was swirling flames of heavenly fire, engulfing the old prophet as he was taken up on the horses of angels.

"My father!"

As John cried out, the image disappeared and he was only aware of himself. His cracked voice echoed off the slime-infected stones around him. This was the birthing chamber of lepers.

Had he not seen the Spirit descend and heard the Voice speaking?

"This is My beloved...listen to Him!"[3]

In the dark he drew into his own spirit and resolved to wait for reassurance. At risk of their own lives, the disciples he had sent again to the Master should be returning by now—unless some greater ill had befallen them.

The Baptist sighed. At last a shameful tear escaped the eye that had beheld Him passing among the throngs coming to be baptized. Not then his cousin. Not his brother from the hearth any longer. Not anymore his junior by half a year, the taunt John had often sent Him in their youth. No. It was He— the Word made flesh and walking in their midst.

Though the words were given sound through his own voice, it was the Spirit who was testifying. And the preacher knew it.

"Behold! The Lamb of God who takes away the sin of the whole world!"[4]

In the distance John heard footfalls descending the stone stairs. His heart seized in hope. They had come back at last with word from the Master, their eyes afire and their warm hands embracing him, bracing him for whatever awaited him here. As the new troubler of Israel, John had no assurance that horses and chariots like those that swept Elijah from this mortal plane would be coming for him.

Stiffly, he sat up trying to smooth his wild hair and beard a bit before his companions were given audience by the jailer. Perhaps they had remembered to bring him a blanket and some bread. The steps approached. Torchlight shone beneath the cell door as the heavy lock turned on its bearing.

The Baptist shielded his eyes that were no longer used to the light. The jailer thrust the greasy lamp into his confines.

"On your feet, Baptist!"

A thick forearm and rough hand grasped the sleeve of his shirt and yanked him onto unsteady feet. Ducking out of the doorway his head came up before the hooded giant. Behind the Goliath's legs for an instant John saw the executioner's blade gleam in the torchlight. They led him away.

Zacharias' song came back as in the days of his youth. His father, an old priest by then, would stroke the hair of his only son, the Lord's answer to Elisabeth's barren womb, and the sound of his father's voice would sing his son to sleep. It seemed John heard him now.

"Shema, Yisrael Adonai Eloheynu Adonai Echad!" Hear O Israel, the Lord our God, the Lord is One!

We have become completely new through the cross of Christ. We were raised up by the Spirit in His resurrection. The spiritual nature and image of Christ Jesus indwells us now. He gives us our new identity. In our new spirit-man, God has constructed His Temple. He is there in the Holy of Holies, and we have access through Christ's blood hour by hour. The new man of glory has been brought home to his Father. If we are agents of recreation, we are messengers of the cross.

The effect of the cross is not only historic. It *is* as God *is*. Past, present, and future, the activity of the cross endures, pro-acting, providing, protecting, and pronouncing a full disclosure of *"I Am that I Am"* (Exod. 3:14 KJV). Eternally, the cross is an unstoppable chain reaction of exponential life-giving. In the cross, Jesus, the Last Adam, became the Life-giving Spirit.

More than two decades ago, our local church body experienced a visitation of the Holy Spirit. It was sovereign, powerful, and life-changing for all who entered the slipstream of His Presence. One glory-filled morning, several people suddenly saw a simultaneous open vision of the cross, tall and bloody, glorious and inviting, planted firmly in the center of the sanctuary. It seemed to gleam with radiant light that changed the evidence of its suffering into the most desirable of emblems. That was the day we realized that the glory we were receiving in that moment was flowing to us from the cross of

Christ in Jerusalem two thousand years ago! People present then still carry the transformation they received that day in the glory revealed in the cross. They still vibrate with that glory.

The truth and effectiveness of the cross is simple enough for a child to enter fully. What happened at the cross when God reconciled the world to Himself is a mystery we shall keep discovering for all eternity. Like the cascading force unleashed in the splitting of an atom, the action of Calvary will be ever unfolding in power. The glory of the cross is an explosive, eternal, energy-creating, continually unfolding revelation of beauty. The cross is the glory of God. In it we behold Him as He really is. Calvary must not be an aversion, or a thing of the past. For as long as we have mortal flesh, as long as we seek His power, we will find Him at the cross. We'll find the power of the Spirit in the blood. Calvary is not the rear view mirror. John looked present and forward through an open door in Heaven and saw the Lamb standing as slain. The writer of Hebrews heard the blood speaking!

Jesus was brought down from the cross, but He has not left it in history as a thing of the past. We mustn't do that either. We live because He died there. He lives because He died there! If we are seeking any other than the Lamb we are looking for another Jesus—other than the One He is. The true Christ in us is the Christ in whom fellowship through suffering brings glory. The Life-giving Spirit will draw us to the cross. All who receive Him are drawn into fellowship in His execution. That is the only liberation. That is the only triumph. The cross is where we become conquerors just as He has:

> *For Your sake we are killed all day long; we are accounted as sheep for the slaughter. Yet in all these things we are more than conquerors through Him who loved us* (Romans 8:36-37).

The blood of Jesus surrounds His Spirit of glory to create a song of redemption that works like atoms splitting. When an atom splits, the core material becomes an uncontainable burst of energy. As it moves ever outward, those moving particles pierce those they make contact with. They are absorbed into the new atom and another explosion occurs. It bursts outward like a flood and repeats the same action in multiplied dimensions all around. It is a good illustration of the glory of the cross, made effective through the blood and brought alive to us by the Spirit. It is power that will change everything that receives it.

When Jesus expired on Calvary, the old era ended. A new age began. It precedes one that is coming. But for now, as we see Him, we see Him through Calvary, and in the power of the Spirit we can walk in His glory. Let us minister that same glory to others. Ultimately, the whole of creation will be filled. Soon the earth will be full of this glory!

FOCAL POINT

In our search for meaning as human beings, we must begin with the Word of God. We must take our compass readings from the Bible exactly as it describes and presents itself: a supernatural revelation both of God and of His design for humankind. The incarnation, crucifixion, resurrection, and ascension of Jesus Christ unveil the ultimate demonstration of both of those realities. Just as without His death the entire mission of God in Christ would have no meaning or effect, so also *the Bible without the cross loses all meaning.*

An instrument of death is the symbol of Christian faith. For believers it is the emblem of glory and victory. The atonement provides victory over sin, death, and the devil, reconciliation to the Father, and power for personal transformation. The predominant view of the cross for the first thousand years of Christian history was as victory. Church father Irenaeus wrote, "The work of Christ is first and foremost a victory over the powers which hold mankind in bondage: sin, death and the devil."[5]

> *They overcame* [satan] *by the blood of the Lamb and the word of their testimony; and they loved not their lives unto the death* (Revelation 12:11).

The cross is the focal point of the entire revelation of Scripture because the purpose of Scripture is to foretell what God had pre-ordained to do in His eternal covenant with the race created in His image. The further intention of Scripture is to record the fulfillment of God's plan and to pass the record forward once Christ revealed it in the flesh.

Before He made the world or anything in it, the Godhead had Calvary in mind. The intention for His man and woman, to subject them (and the rest of creation) to futility while devising a perfect mechanism of total redemption in order to bring them back to Himself, could only be accomplished one way: through the Lamb slain before the foundation of the world. From prehistory, the cross is the central event of the history of the world.

FULLNESS OF GLORY

So let's look at Calvary in the cosmic sense. What really happened there? The New Testament Scriptures sum up the achievement of Calvary in three words: salvation, revelation, and conquest. At the cross, the Son of God rescued us, fully disclosed Himself, and overcame evil. God was moved by the perfection of His holy love. That is the heart of the cross. That is the glory of God. His completely complete work has made provision for every aspect of human life. Through His blood, Jesus made propitiation for sin, paid the purchase price for our redemption, provided justification of grace just-as-if I'd never sinned, and reconciled us to the Father.

> *Herein is love, not that we loved God, but that He loved us, and sent His Son to be the propitiation for our sins* (1 John 4:10 KJV).

This is the aspect of our lives that applies to our temple court life. Propitiation is the placating of wrath. It recalls images of the Tabernacle and the "blame" or *hattat* offering. Blood was the only sacrifice considered effective for the contaminating effects of sin. Anything impure, less than perfect, having any shadow of imperfection whatsoever was understood to carry a radioactive-like power that would arouse the wrath of God and drive away the Presence from the Tent of Meeting. Jesus is our blame offering. His cross decontaminates us, cleansing the temple and bidding His Presence to come. The glory of the cross is the revelation that God who demands a sacrifice on the basis that light cannot fellowship with darkness, provided the sacrifice in Himself. *"The Son of God did not come to be served, but to serve, and to give His life a ransom for many"* (Mark 10:45).

"In whom we have redemption through His blood, the forgiveness of sins, according to the riches of His grace" (Eph. 1:7 KJV). To redeem is to buy back in the market place either as a purchase price or ransom. Redemption speaks to our plight as sinners—that we needed saving and we could not save ourselves. We needed Someone who could pay the price to purchase us back from slavery. Israel's redemption from Egypt was costly in that it required a great exertion of power. We see that in the ten plagues of judgment and miracles God wrought to redeem His people. Redemption expends holy energy in a way no human may understand. Without the purchase price fully paid, the transaction to extricate us from captivity and transfer us from

darkness to the kingdom of light could never have taken effect. But as it is, through the cross we have radical deliverance from sin and guilt.

> *God presented Him as a sacrifice of atonement, through faith in His blood. He did this to demonstrate His justice, because in His forbearance He had left the sins committed beforehand unpunished—He did it to demonstrate His justice at the present time, so as to be just and the one who justifies those who have faith in Jesus* (Romans 3:25-26 NIV).

Justification is our legal standing before a judge. In an act of justice, we have been acquitted in the court of heaven. To be justified is not cloaking our unrighteousness in Christ's righteousness. It's providing proof of evidence that we are not deserving of the penalty of sin. We know that nothing we have done, however good, makes us deserving of full acquittal for every wrong we have done. The source of our acquittal is God's grace. The basis of it is His blood. In an act of justice on the cross, God condemned sin to the death penalty. In grace, Christ died our death. The evidence He brought into court is His blood—innocent blood, without the slightest forensic evidence of sin. The effect of this justice is membership in His covenant community.

> *And all things are of God, who hath reconciled us to Himself by Jesus Christ, and hath given to us the ministry of reconciliation; To wit, that God was in Christ, reconciling the world unto Himself, not imputing their trespasses unto them; and hath committed unto us the word of reconciliation* (2 Corinthians 5:18-19 KJV).

The fourth aspect of our salvation affected at Calvary is reconciliation—reunion with our heavenly Father. This is the most personal one. We have come home. The relationship that once was when God had us in mind before creation, before sin, but was broken when sin entered the human race through Adam, has been restored. Reconciliation means we have peace with God through the blood. We have been adopted as sons and made heirs of His riches through the exchange at Calvary. And it means we have access of active communion with God as Christ does. Christ calls Him "Abba" Daddy! And so He is our Daddy, too. Now we understand just a bit of why we glory in the cross of Christ. Glory!

ENABLED BY GLORY

The cross enables us to begin to see God as He really is, for it is there that His true nature is demonstrated—the nature of self-giving without reserve, without end, without demand, and without strings attached. Calvary is the climax of Jesus' mission to earth. There He embraced the sin that had alienated the human race from God and one another. There He returned us to our Father. There He made us His brothers and sisters in this world and the one to come. Pride and a self-serving nature is the foundation of the kingdom of darkness. Against that darkness Christ hurled Himself as the penalty for man's departure from God. He came down so that we might go up. He came here to be with us so that we might be with Him in His Kingdom.

Who can resist such love? This love includes judgment of all that we are, have been, and will be, and yet it extends to us freedom from condemnation. What occurred on the cross released power overwhelming enough to completely undo the systems of this world and the spiritual kingdom of darkness. Like two sides of a coin, the cross and the glory are one. Together they shine out, fully reflecting the face of Christ into our hearts.

God's glory is not a caprice of the Deity by which He keeps His creation hanging by a thread of desire. It bursts out all over His creation. When we look at the miracles of Jesus according to the timing and manner of their occurrence, we see they are often purposed to be specific demonstrations of His glory: the man healed as he washed in Siloam, and the sickness, death, and resurrection of Lazarus. Jesus nearly always defined the timing and manner of His miracles, together with the distress and suffering on the part of the persons involved, "for the glory of God."

We are not talking about the glory *plus* something such as obedience or healing power. The glory alone is enough. A few years ago one of our church families called us. Their mother had suddenly become ill and had been taken to the hospital while she was visiting family out of town. The tests at the hospital indicated there was a shadow on her brain, and she was being transferred to a larger regional medical facility for further testing. I (Mahesh) prayed, and heard the Lord say, "I will overshadow her." I told the dear mother, "The shadow of the Most High is going to overshadow that shadow on your brain." It was the word from the glory in the power of the cross. The next day, doctors did another MRI. There was no more shadow or any other indication of a problem. It had simply disappeared.

Where did such authority come from? The shadow of the cross. The cross has made every provision, mortal and eternal, that a man or woman will ever need, physically, spiritually, emotionally, and intellectually. Surely this is the central location where the glory of God begins. God, grant us to enter the cross and so find ourselves abiding in Your full glory.

THE CROSS OPENS THE DOOR

When you are in the glory of God, you feel as if your skin is smiling! We experience God's glory in a way similar to a child being overwhelmed by unexpected goodness, kindness, generosity, or the spectacle of a wonderful event like receiving a marvelous gift.

The Holy Spirit makes God's glory evident and effectual. Jesus' death, burial, resurrection, and ascension opened the door for the full revelation of God's glory. After what happened in the Garden of Eden, the cross is the only plausible way to restore the glory of God to the human race that bears His image. Every effect has a cause and every cause an effect. The glory of God experienced in His creation is the pure effect of Calvary. Without Calvary there could be no salvation, no resurrection, and no glory. There had to be a viable and certain death of the old, sin-tarnished cosmos so a new glorious one could be born. The work of the cross opened the way.

The cross of Christ is not a past-tense event. It is still happening! The power of the cross is present and effectual. It opens the way to glory in both Heaven and earth. Think about what John saw in his revelation. The saints in glory were utterly whole. They were worshiping the Lamb who appeared as having been slain (see Rev. 5). In His resurrected body, Jesus showed hard-to-convince Thomas the marks of the cross.

So at Calvary we see God's blood and His glory together. When God covered the nakedness of Adam and Eve in the Garden, He made them clothing out of the skins of slain animals. Blood made provision where glory had been lost. It pointed the way to a renewal, a return to communion, a rebirth foreshadowed in the covenant with Moses.

Deep in the interior of Moses' Tent of Meeting rested the Mercy Seat. The Ark of the Covenant was the place in which two elements mingled in the demonstration and manifestation of God. It was His throne in the earth. There, the High Priest sprinkled the blood of atonement. And there the glory rested. Out of that living presence, God would speak to His people. There, the Presence of God was a dewy pillar of cloud by day and shining fire through the night. Authority and power to dispossess Israel's enemies emanated from the glory. At the same time the glory provided food and water. But access could only be had with shed blood present and working through the atoning sacrifice perpetually offered at the throne.

Dancing with Glory

Glory is not an *it*. The glory of God is the Presence of a Person, the Lord of Glory. We can enter His glory and in it become congruent with Him. Then we can bring others with us. It is not just for the sake of personal experience or revelation. His glory is meant to be shared. We become ambassadors of glory. It is there in the glory that miracles dwell.

In the early years as I (Mahesh) came to know the power of the Spirit and started to share the love of Christ, people started sharing with me their desperate prayer needs. About this time, as I wrote in my book, *Only Love Can Make a Miracle*, a man named Galen, who was an elder in a local Methodist church, told me about Drew, a little boy from his church. Drew was four years old. He had been born with a congenital heart defect that had required open-heart surgery. While this surgery is fairly common today, at the time it was very new and very risky. Drew was not expected to live.

His parents had heard about me and asked if I would be willing to pray for their son. They did not ask me to come pray with him in person, simply that I pray for him. Naturally, I told Galen that I would be more than glad to pray for this little boy, and I did, right on the spot.

As soon as I began to pray, I had a vision of the Lord. It wasn't just a mental image. My eyes were open, and I saw Him standing there with a little child in His arms. As I watched, He gave a slight gesture with His hand, as if He were signaling to someone. Somehow, in the context of the vision, I understood that He was signaling for music to begin.

Then He began to dance. Holding the little boy close against His breast, He danced around and around, laughing merrily. I saw that the little boy was laughing too. I could not hear the music, but I saw them dancing and laughing together for what seemed like several minutes. Then the vision ended.

I really didn't know what to make of what I had seen. Did the vision mean that the little boy would be healed? Or was it a picture of Jesus receiving him into Heaven? I decided not to try to interpret it. I just told Galen what I had seen and asked him to relate the vision to Drew's parents. All this happened on a Tuesday.

On Friday of that week, little Drew died. I was greatly saddened by the news. My heart really went out to his family. His parents invited me to his funeral. It was the first time I had met them. Despite their loss, they were radiant. They hugged me and said, "We just want you to know that your vision is what is sustaining us through this." They invited me to their home the next week to meet some of their friends. They wanted me to tell them what I had seen when I prayed for Drew.

At their home, I described the vision as I had seen it. Then the father got up. "I would like to share something with all of you," he said. "Because Drew was born with a heart defect, he couldn't be like other children. He couldn't do the things they could do. All day long he would lie in his crib, waiting for his daddy to come home. When I would get home, I would put on his favorite music, pick him up from his crib, and dance all around the room with him. As I would dance, he would laugh and laugh. It was his favorite part of the day. Mine, too."

"I never told Mahesh about this. But when he had his vision, we realized exactly what it meant. We knew that when Drew passed away, Jesus was going to take over right where we had left off. That's the only reason we've been able to come through this terrible ordeal the way we have."

Over the years in times of crisis, the reality of this vision and the story of little Drew and the dancing Jesus has come back to me again and again. When we begin to know Jesus Christ in His glory, He wipes away our tears. May the Lord open our ears to hear the rhythms of glory that are all around us. The reality of the living Christ is available to us through the shed blood of Calvary. We can become one with the vibration of His presence. God wants to bring us to a place where, in the midst of pain and heartbreak, we can hear the harmony of Heaven and pick it up now. One day we shall see Him face to face, and it is my anticipation that on that glorious day of the marriage supper of the Lamb there will be a divine waltz where Christ will come and take His Bride in His arms, and we will dance together in everlasting glory.

EVERYTHING TRANSFORMED

Throughout the language of Scripture, "the glory" belongs directly to the Lord. The glory is intimately God's. The glory never occurs apart from Him. His glory is always revealed in God Himself. His glory precedes and lingers after Him in evidence of His presence. Think of the lingering fragrance of expensive perfume after the one wearing it embraces you, or of the lasting image of a bright light in your eye after the flash of a camera. The experience is the imprint of the previous one, and is itself an experience. The glory is representative of and intrinsic to God because His glory is the demonstration of His Being. The glory should be recognized as indicating He is present and He is working.

The atmosphere of God's glory is an ongoing, abiding visitation. It is an enjoyable "place" in which everything comes into harmony:

> *The wolf shall dwell with the lamb, and the leopard shall lie down with the young goat, and the calf and the lion and the fattened calf together; and a little child shall lead them... They shall not hurt or destroy in all my holy mountain; for the earth shall be full of the knowledge of the Lord as the waters cover the sea* (Isaiah 11:6,9 ESV).

In the glory, light overwhelms darkness, hope overwhelms despair, joy supersedes mourning, and faith exiles unbelief. The Spirit of God settles down in rest and invites us to enter His glory. The place of the glory is always a place where Jesus is recognized, welcomed, exalted, and worshiped. His name is Emmanuel, *"God with us"* (Matt. 1:23).

Isaiah continues:

> *In that day the root of Jesse, who shall stand as a signal for the peoples—of Him shall the nations inquire, and His resting place shall be glorious. In that day the Lord will extend His hand yet a second time to recover the remnant that remains of His people...* (Isaiah 11:10-11).

And so our hearts cry, "Show us Your glory!"

What is the secret of this glory? It is the mystery of the ages that is being revealed to us. It's the Root of Jesse and the Spirit who rests on Him. To know Jesus as He is, we must know Him by the Spirit. We must know Him through the cross: "The crucifixion settled who and what we are."[6] The crucified Son makes us individuals, and then integrates us with others who know Him. Our new nature finds its fullness outside of self as a member of a community of people who have been redeemed by the blood of the Lamb. Through the cross we become a community of celebration.

Because the cross is the singular demonstration of the overwhelming mercy of God, it remains the key to experiencing the glory of God. The cross reveals God as He is. It shows Him perfect, self-giving, irresistible, humble, absolutely omnipotent in power—and completely obsessed with His love for us.

We must know Him as Crucified and Living—hour by hour. The Spirit of His Glory has awakened us to intimate communion knowledge of Him as He is, and we are changed. We see the Lamb and we recognize that He is *slain and standing* in the throne of our hearts. He is *in us* just as He is in Heaven. Full of majesty, He reigns through us in love and recreates everything in us to say, "Glory!"

The Bible has as many references to glory as there are days in a year. There is glory for every day! In the book of Romans alone, seventeen verses speak of different facets of the glory of our salvation. Altogether they present a dynamic litany to the glory of God:

There is the glory of the immortal ways. "[They] *exchanged the* **glory** *of the immortal God for images resembling mortal man and birds and animals and creeping things"* (Rom. 1:23 ESV).

There is the glory of eternal life. *"...to those who by patience in well-doing seek for* **glory** *and honor and immortality, He will give eternal life"* (Rom. 2:7 ESV).

There is glory for doing "good" in obedience to faith that brings salvation. *"...but **glory** and honor and peace for everyone who does good, the Jew first and also the Greek"* (Rom. 2:10 ESV).

There is glory of God's truth. *"God's truth abounds to his **glory**..."* (Rom. 3:7 ESV).

There is the glory of faith toward God and His promise. *"No distrust made him waver concerning the promise of God, but he grew strong in his faith as he gave **glory** to God"* (Rom. 4:20 ESV).

There is the glory of hope in God. *"Through Him we have also obtained access by faith into this grace in which we stand, and we rejoice in hope of the **glory** of God"* (Rom. 5:2 ESV).

There is the glory of the Father that raised Christ from the dead. *"We were buried therefore with Him by baptism into death, in order that, just as Christ was raised from the dead by the **glory** of the Father, we too might walk in newness of life"* (Rom. 6:4 ESV).

There is the glory that will be revealed in us. *"For I consider that the sufferings of this present time are not worth comparing with the **glory** that is to be revealed to us"* (Rom. 8:18 ESV).

There is the glory of the freedom of the children of God. *"Creation itself will be set free from its bondage to corruption and obtain the freedom of the **glory** of the children of God"* (Rom. 8:21 ESV).

There is glory of having been justified through Christ's exchange, that is made righteous just-as-if I'd never sinned. *"And those whom He predestined He also called, and those whom He called He also justified, and those whom He justified He also **glorified**"* (Rom. 8:30).

There is the glory that belongs to Israel. *"They are Israelites, and to them belong the adoption, the **glory**, the covenants, the giving of the law, the worship, and the promises"* (Rom. 9:4 ESV).

There is the glory that has been prepared in advance for all those who have received God's mercy. *"...that He might make known* *the riches of His **glory** on the vessels of mercy, which He had prepared beforehand for glory"* (Rom. 9:23).

There is the eternal glory of Him from whom, through whom, and to whom all things exist. *"For of Him and through Him and to Him are all things, to whom be **glory** forever"* (Rom. 11:36).

There is the glory of God's mercy shown to the Gentiles. *"...that the Gentiles might **glorify** God for His mercy"* (Rom. 15:9).

There is the glory of God's wisdom shown through Jesus Christ. *"To the only wise God be **glory** forevermore through Jesus Christ!"* (Rom. 16:27).

There is the glory of unity in Christ. *"...that you may with one mind and one mouth **glorify** the God and Father of our Lord Jesus Christ"* (Rom. 15:6).

There is the glory of receiving one another as Christ has received each of us. *"Therefore receive one another, just as Christ also received us, to the **glory** of God"* (Rom. 15:7).

All that glory is revealed in just one book of the Bible! When we begin to speak of the glory, we begin to understand that the glory of God is a manifold Presence of the Spirit of God at work. The Holy Spirit is our closest Companion. He has been sent out to find the perfect bride for the Son of God. Daily, He is Present to refresh and guide us, to strengthen and encourage us. He should not be neglected. He deserves your worship. He is present to fulfill the ministry of Christ in you. The Spirit is working to build the corporate Body of Christ into the full stature of a perfect man like unto the Son of God. And He is busy lovingly and excitedly preparing a bride for the soon-coming Bridegroom. He is called the glory of the Father and He is residing within you.

ENDNOTES

1.   From *The Dream of the Rood,* lines 1-13. Translation copyright © 1982, Jonathan A. Glenn. Used by permission. For the

complete poem as translated from Old English, see http://www.lightspill.com/poetry/oe/rood.html.

2. Isa. 40:3-5 NASB.

3. Matt. 17:5 ESV.

4. John 1:29.

5. Gustav Aulen, *Christus Victor* (1930; SPCK, 1931), 22-23.

6. Robert W. Jenson, *Systematic Theology, Vol. 1: The Triune God* (New York, NY: Oxford University Press, 1997), 189.

CHAPTER 2

FROM INSIDE
OUT—FROM OUTSIDE IN

I saw glory's tree
honored with trappings, shining with joys,
decked with gold; gems had
wrapped that forest tree worthily round.
Yet through that gold I clearly perceived
old strife of wretches, when first it began
to bleed on its right side....
I saw that doom-beacon turn trappings and hews:
sometimes with water wet,
drenched with blood's going; sometimes
with jewels decked.[1]

He loved him. And He understood him—though I think that Judas never accepted that He did. I, John, was witness from the beginning.

I wonder if the man who had charge of our moneybox was always just a thief at heart, struggling with his own desperate insistence on making his mark and ready to steal every opportunity that came along. Not unlike the rest of us, I suppose. But he let it get the upper hand. I suspect the betrayer was double-minded until that night; perhaps he was uncertain until the very end.

The zealot was more appealing in some ways than all the rest of us. Passionate and apt to catch a crowd and persuade them. But he was insecure. Even the Lord's unfailing love could not break through that callus. He would have made the fittest of apostles eventually except for that. It was as though Judas could not trust himself to the faithfulness of another, not even God. And in the end he was unfaithful himself. He stayed until he finished his course. Until he had betrayed Him.

No one saw it coming beforehand except the two of them, Jesus and Judas himself. Looking back, I wonder how we all could have missed it. I had been uneasy in Judas' presence from time to time. He tried to persuade the Master with impassioned arguments that Jesus should allow the throngs coming out to see Him to anoint Him king in Israel.

In the end it was she, a woman among the servers, who did it. That night at the table at Simon's, just five nights before Pesach.

The schism was complete. I think I saw it on him as it entered Judas' heart at last. My eyes met Luke's. He was watching, too, and we spoke of it once later. With clear, sad eyes, the Lord looked at His own disciple across the table, their hands still dripping oil and a drop of it on Judas' lip.

"Do it quickly," Jesus said quietly.

Christ's words offended as they indicted. He never tried to impose a different course upon the man He called His friend.

"He who comes up another way, the same is a thief and robber."

He used to tell us things like that. The Master knew who amongst us would betray Him. Peter was afraid of himself until Jesus came to us after the grave. By then it was too late for Judas.

I wonder if we could have ever received Judas back unless the Lord in His glory had set him in our midst and made it so. We had our differences even at the end. Yet we were all handpicked, weren't we? Hadn't He handpicked even Judas to come with us? We all partook of miracles.

The woman came suddenly in upon us. In her hands that box of alabaster and its contents—her dowry—the whole prospect of her future. That box contained the only guarantee she possessed for herself as a bride, a wife, a mother—for a woman in our time.

And she spent it all on Him without a thought. Without a care. With gleaming eyes and her face as of an angel, she poured it out upon Him.

Her sister was disapproving of that waste as were we. Martha was always so practical and attentive, tirelessly looking to our needs. The hospitality of the house in Bethany drew us often. They would cheerfully accommodate us all. We did cause quite a scene in the days after their brother was raised up from his tomb. In the presence of the mourners, Lazarus came stumbling out, his grave clothes still tightly wound.

We had so much to learn.

The Rabbi's voice was full of meaning, resonate with joy and the fear of the Lord whenever He tried to explain things to us. As the days of the feast grew nearer, I grew increasingly uneasy. By then something had begun to tell me that darkness would come before deliverance.

There was a boisterous stir about the waste as we witnessed what Mary had done. The fragrance of her perfume filled our senses, as satiating as the food we had taken in, as intoxicating as our wine. It all happened so fast. Jesus burst out laughing and told us all to leave the woman alone.

"It's for My burial."[2] He pushed his hands through His locks, dripping with the dew of her evening offering. The redolence filled the entire house; it was so rich, so expensive!

The smell of her oil was still on Him even after our *mikva* as He presided over our Pesach table five nights later. I suppose it gave Him some comfort that He had with Him those who loved Him fully, although we didn't understand all He said or did.

The woman was unashamed even after we all judged her a fool. Our collective opining had a righteous air. I realize now that she was the discerning one. Hers was the righteous act. We all supported Judas as we derided her. We who had wagged our heads at the Pharisees when they would stand on the corners of the high street displaying their piety with loud voices and sad faces.

That night we raised our voices and thrust out our hands to stop her as if we cried out for the poor. Really, we were thinking of our own provision. We depended on what came into the box Judas kept for us.

Mary's box contained more treasure than all. Her gift was more support for His cause than anything our moneybox had ever held. We saw His glory that night as we had so many times before, and every time it took us by surprise. Just as it did that night at Simon, the leper's.

The night He was anointed.

In our congregation we have an elderly woman who has been adopted as our spiritual grandmother. At one-hundred years old, she stands approximately four feet tall, but in the Spirit, Elena is taller and mightier than Goliath. Spanish is her native tongue and English her adopted one. But prayer is Elena's mother tongue. When you are near her, her gentle spirit and frail body seem to shine with the power of God. Literally. For some time now, if you sit beside her, you will see softly glinting on her skin and in her clothes tiny, bright silver flecks, sometimes brighter, sometimes more faint. What is it? Where does it come from? Why is it there? We don't know. The presence of the Lord is so tangible when you are with her that it seems natural to see the shining glory of God as radiant and abiding in her physical body as it is in her inner being.

The appearance of the glory of God in the Gospels is described as bright illumination, such as in the physical appearance of angels and of Christ in His transfiguration and after His resurrection. We cannot speak of the glory of God without thinking of bright light—and without personalizing it. Jesus prophesied through David, *"I will tell of Your name to my brethren; in the midst of the assembly I will praise You"* (Ps. 22:22 NASB; also Heb. 2:12). The Hebrew word for praise is *halal,* and means "to shine, to flash forth light," or to glorify.[3] When He comes home to His Temple, His glory illuminates His surroundings. The glory appeared as angels sang to announce the Savior's birth. The Word Incarnate revealed His glory when He took on human flesh and walked on earth as an ordinary person among ordinary people. His glory is *"full of grace and truth"* (John 1:14).

In the Gospels, satan tests Jesus by showing Him the glory of the world's kingdoms. Satan offers their power and wealth to Christ. He refuses. The New Testament centers the manifestation of God's glory in persons' lives. First, in the Son of God through His character and example of obedience and devotion to His Father in Heaven; and then through those who put their trust in Him and in His blood for their salvation. Jesus is coming in the glory of His Father (see Luke 9:26). It will be a day of great power experienced by the whole world and by all who have ever lived. The Gospels call it the Day of the Lord (see Mark 13:26).

The martyr Stephen testifies that it was the glory that appeared to Abraham and called him on the journey to the land of God's promise (see Acts 7:2). Glory as the face of an angel rested on Stephen and convicted his stoners as he was being killed (see Acts 7:54-60). The Corinthian letters call woman the glory of man and point to the creation of woman in a prefiguring of God creating the human race as the helpmate of His Son (see 1 Cor. 11). Paul speaks of the resurrection as the fulfillment and beginning of glory for everyone washed in the blood and having the Spirit of God. He says the glory of the ministry of the Spirit will culminate in so much greater glory than the shining face of Moses after he came down from Sinai. He says that glory was the ministry of death, and we have the ministry of life that comes from the Lord who is the Spirit (see 2 Cor. 3:11-18).

The first time I (Bonnie) saw the flecks of shining golden stuff that has come to be associated with "the glory" was fourteen years prior to this writing. Mahesh and I were at a small gathering to honor an elderly minister. I noticed from across the room that Mahesh had something glinting on his cheek just below his left eye. The thing became a distraction to me, so I moved across the room and plucked it off. A few moments later, I noticed the glint again and removed what I thought must be another piece of glitter. It happened again and I plucked it off and examined it more closely. It was thin and fine and bright, and the look of it gave me a feeling inside like a happy sigh. I had not seen or heard of anything like this before, but it seemed that whatever it was, it had emerged from within, exuding from some essence internal to Mahesh's body.

We began to experience this more and more. One of the most memorable times occurred as we sat at our family dinner table with Sister Ruth Heflin. She said, "You know, I feel we should just sing." She took the hands of two of our children and began to worship the Lord in her inimitable way. The nearness of Jesus was intimate and powerful. At the end of the song, Ruth was covered with a film of glistening, golden something. It had come from within as we had worshiped together.

For us, these appearances have never been something that take our focus away from God; rather, they intensify our focus upon the immediate Presence of the Lord and what He desires to communicate in that moment. They are a tiny glimpse of the immediacy of His Person with us and His unfathomable riches and treasures.

LOOK FOR THE GLORY

About thirty years ago, a few days after we had our first child, the doctors found that he had terminal kidney disease. Ben was already dying, and there was nothing anybody could do. There we were, serving the Lord, our lives totally devoted to pouring ourselves out to God and His people, and our first child was dying. I (Mahesh) had read about people's hair turning white overnight from stress, but I didn't really believe it—until I was in such extreme distress myself. I went to take a morning shower, and I saw that the hair on my chest had turned gray overnight. The intensity of the distress had affected me chemically.

But the Lord was setting us up for perhaps one of the most outstanding miracles in our lives. As our newborn son Ben lay in the ICU, screaming in excruciating pain after multiple surgeries and still no breakthrough in sight, Bonnie and I prayed in the waiting area, "Oh Lord, let the power of your blood speak for Ben." Shortly after that prayer, the nurse came running out to us, urging us to come see our son right away. I thought, "This is it. Our son has gone home to be with the Lord." Instead, she said, "I don't know what is happening." Tears were streaming down her face as she led us to his room. The glory was there surrounding our son's broken body as a cloud of golden light. Ben had his arm extended and a look of total peace on his tiny face. The blood shed at Calvary created a song, a presence of the Lord around our son, and in a mystery connected Ben to the cross outside the city of Jerusalem 2,000 years ago. The words of Isaiah spoken generations before the events of Calvary came to pass in Ben's body in front of our eyes: "He has carried our sorrows, He has taken our pains" (see Isa. 53:4). Ben was sleeping peacefully. The monitor still indicated his body was in crisis and spasms of pain, but in a mystery of the glory, because of the blood, Ben had entered into the song of the Lord, his body had picked up the vibration of God, and all the pain fled in the presence of the voice of glory. That was the beginning of the miracle of Ben's total healing, and his testimony continues to bring God glory.

That miracle became the seed for miracles as we have shared it now with millions of people around the world. For example, one night when I was in Kinshasa, the capital city of the Democratic Republic of Congo, I felt that God said, "Tell your story." I simply told the story of Ben, and I said, "And God came and healed him; the glory came and healed him."[4] I told them that in John 8:58, Jesus Christ of Nazareth said, *"before Abraham was, I Am,"* that He is the Lord that heals you, and that today you can call upon the name of the Lord for salvation and healing. That evening more than fifty thousand people (out of a crowd of nearly four hundred thousand) made a decision for Jesus Christ, simply because He is *"the same yesterday, today, and forever"* (Heb. 13:8). That night I remember the Holy Spirit coming to me and asking, "Was it worth it?" Yes, to see fifty thousand people come to Christ in one night from one story of healing and redemption was worth it.

We read in the King James Version of Psalm 4: *"Hear me when I call, O God of my righteousness: Thou hast enlarged me when I was in distress."* When you are in distress, it is a setup for enlargement. It is important, therefore, in your times of distress, to enlarge your focus. Do not focus on your loss; focus on what you have left. Above all, focus on the Lord Himself, whose presence will take care of everything. He tells us, *"I will never leave you nor forsake you"* (Heb. 13:5; see also Deut. 31:6, 8; Josh. 1:5).

The Lord is with you. But you've got to commune with Him. How can you do that? Ever since the blood of Jesus was shed, you have been made one with Him. You can come and have access. But often we maintain a kind of religious separation—God is there, I am here. Yet the Lord wants us to commune and have communion. Through the blood, God draws us to enter into this amazing communion of the Father, Son, and Holy Spirit. There is an intense, awesome union with Him that is experienced while not fully comprehended. God is allowing us to enter into intimate communion and eternal partnership with the Three in One.

This is where we begin to look for the glory of the Lord. Jesus told the believers to tarry in Jerusalem until they were endued with power from on high and they received the Holy Spirit on Pentecost. To this day, we have been made partakers of the Holy Spirit. It is wonderful, but most of us have only experienced 0.1 percent of the awesomeness of the glory God has for us. He wants us to enter into much, much more. So much that we begin to see His face.

"Beholding as in a mirror the glory of the Lord, we are being transformed from glory to glory" (2 Cor. 3:18). There is a "secret place" where His glory is. No plague shall come near your dwelling when you are in the secret place of the Most High (see Ps. 91:10). When times of challenge come, times of distress, let them push you more into God! Let yourself be drawn into the secret place of His glorious presence revealed.

SECRET PLACE OF GLORY

A while ago, we got a call from a pastor friend in another state. He was crying on the phone, and in the intensive care unit with one of the families from his church. Their teenage daughter was dying because her liver was failing. Although there was remote hope for a liver transplant in another state, everyone was in total distress. She had taken too many pills, and they were toxic.

When we got off the phone, we went straight to prayer. It was as if we entered a bubble of His glory, and while we were there, it was as if the Lord took us with Him into the very cells of the girl's liver. That sounds weird, but it was something like that. And we did not come out until the liver was healthy and clean, which was about twenty-six hours later. For twenty-six hours, we carried the situation into the presence of the Lord, and His glory surrounded it.

We did not lock ourselves into an empty room for that whole time. We were at home, going about our normal activities, including sleeping, while we carried the situation in intercession. Then the Lord said, "It is done. Phone her mother and her pastor."

When we called, the doctors were just coming in to talk to the family, saying, "We had nothing to do with this. We don't know why, but the liver is better than normal." It was totally healed.

In the secret place of the Most High, you can breathe in the atmosphere of miracles. In that place, the Lord wants to strengthen us and heal our children. Times of intensity and challenge and distress push us right into His glory. From that time on, it is not you by yourself, but it is you plus the Lord. All of us may be in an ash heap from time to time, but the Lord wants to bring us into enlargement.

WEIGHTY GLORY

One of our Zion College students came up with an interesting statement. He said, "Glory and gold are measured in weight, and the Bible calls the afflictions of this present age featherweight."

That makes you think. The Bible says, *"the sufferings of this present time are not worthy to be compared with the glory which shall be revealed in us"* (Rom. 8:18). This statement was made by a man who was beaten, stoned, imprisoned, persecuted, and eventually beheaded for the glory of the Gospel.

The Hebrew word for glory is *kabowd*. It means "to be heavy" or weighty.[5] Like gold, the word also implies riches and honor. The glory of God is true riches and it rests in that culture of honor. Picture the glory of the Lord like gold bars stacked on one side of a scale. Now counterbalance the other side with feathers. That's how the challenges in your life now compare to the glory that's coming.

"This momentary, light affliction is producing for us an eternal weight of glory far beyond all comparison" (2 Cor. 4:17 NASB).

Our last enemy, which is death, has been defeated. All other ones are vanquished, and God is reviving and restoring His Church. Western Christians have been talked down to, pampered and plasticized. Our theology and our expectation concerning salvation is anemic—it has lost the power of the blood! We have allowed ourselves to be dumbed-down and willing to live on crumbs. It's an "entitlement generation" that insists: The proof that God is with me is (1) I am going to be rich, (2) I am not going to have any enemies, and (3) I am not going to suffer. Such a life is not portrayed in the Bible. Jesus didn't model it. The glory of the cross is its power to stand in the face of trouble and rise above it. You want to connect with the glory of the cross and live in its shadow by its power. Your moments of difficulty are central locations where God delights to break through. There He often shows you His glory, and when He does you will be changed forever. You are being transformed from inside out!

God has made a vacancy that only you can fill. He has appointed you to become a point of contact between His glory and the world around you. Nobody can do it for you.

> *The eyes of the Lord run to and fro throughout the whole earth, to shew Himself strong in the behalf of them whose heart is perfect toward Him* (2 Chronicles 16:9 KJV).

He is looking for a faith-response on your part. He is looking for supernatural people in natural bodies who live in a natural world. He's longing for a people who can pick up His vibration and transmit His presence wherever they are. The victory is already here. It's our job to make it practical, bringing order out of chaos and releasing Heaven on earth. That's Kingdom glory.

The Spirit of the Living God within each one of us makes Jesus available every way, every day. With the apostle Paul, we can say:

> *I now rejoice in my sufferings for you, and fill up in my flesh what is lacking in the afflictions of Christ, for the sake of His body, which is the church, of which I became a minister according to the stewardship from God which was given to me for you, to fulfill the word of God, the mystery which has been hidden from ages and from generations, but now has been revealed to His saints. To them God willed to make known what are the riches of the glory of this mystery among the Gentiles: which is Christ in you, the hope of glory* (Colossians 1:24-27).

EMANANT

When Jesus spoke of the glory of God, He was speaking of the ministry of the Holy Spirit. This revelation is Personal. He referred to the glory as being directly related to the immediate, intimate activity of God Himself. The glory is the *effulgence* of the Lord as He is present, active, and making Himself known. In the 1913 Webster's Revised Unabridged Dictionary the word that may best define glory as it is used in the Bible is *emanant*. It means issuing or flowing forth; passing forth into an act, or making itself apparent by an effect as in an improvised, often spontaneous spectacle or performance, especially one involving audience participation.[6] This is the perfect word to describe the manifestation of the brightness of glory that emanates from Jesus.

Jesus referred to the glory of God as being demonstrated in miracles and God's holy intervention in human affairs. He used *glory* to describe His personal redemptive mission that would reach a climax in His crucifixion and resurrection. He called that His hour of glory. The glory is the outshining of God's substantive Person. It is the demonstration of His nature as He is. The cross is the demonstration of His nature. From the cross, God's self-giving perfection shines down on us. In his revelation, John saw the Lamb standing in the midst of a throne surrounded by a glorious rainbow. The emerald rainbow is the refraction of the Light of the world. The glorious rainbow, present and visible, emanates from the One who is ruling from His Throne.

> *He who sat there was like a jasper and a sardius stone in appearance; and there was a rainbow around the throne, in appearance like an emerald* (Revelation 4:3).

Jesus Christ is *"the image of the invisible God"* (Col. 1:15). He is *"the brightness of His glory and the express image of His person"* (Heb. 1:3). When we experience His glory, whether as a fiery cloud or through acts of intervention in the natural realm in miracles, signs, and wonders, we don't worship the miracle, we worship the One from whom it comes. We celebrate the demonstration of His presence. Jesus referred to "seeing" the glory of God in terms of miracles and the work of redemption through His cross and resurrection. He spoke of the glory of God in terms of His return to earth and the end of the age when He will mete out justice to His enemies and reward His friends. He used the glory to describe acts and ideas that confounded His detractors. He said He had the glory in Himself in order to reveal it to the world. You will see His glory as you see Him more clearly.

When Jacob lay down in the desert one dark night with nothing but a stone for a pillow, he dreamed a most wondrous dream. A ladder rose into Heaven and angels went up and down from him to God and back again (see Gen. 28). That night, Jacob was touched by the glory. It lingered upon him, transforming and conforming him, beginning inside out. The glory followed Jacob all the way into exile and all the way back home. It was present the night Jacob wrestled with the Angel of the Lord. What a match! When Jacob got up off the mat, he was limping. But he walked away with a great blessing. His identity and his destiny had been changed! But the glory on Jacob didn't stop there. It ran ahead of him to touch the heart of his brother and reconcile the family to one another.

The glory of God is like that. His glory emanates from His person. The glory is as uncontainable as God Himself. The biblical writers all claimed that His glory fills and ultimately fulfills all of creation. The Seraphim who dwell in God's presence are constantly shouting, *"the whole earth is full of His glory!"* (Isa. 6:3). The psalmist David wrote, *"The heavens declare the glory of God"* (Ps. 19:1). The prophet Habakkuk said, *"the earth will be filled with the knowledge of the glory of the Lord as the waters cover the sea"* (Hab. 2:14). God transcends time and material. His glory infuses physical space, and rearranges the order of natural creation, to bring forth miracles in supernatural demonstration of His presence.

CENTER STAGE

The spectacle of Golgotha stands center stage for men and angels, demons, principalities and powers in all ages. What happened outside the gate of Jerusalem two thousand years ago is still unfolding. The cross is a spiritual mission in natural history creating a human spectacle of supernatural achievement. The absolute completeness of Jesus' atoning work was done according to non-negotiable conditions of righteousness that issues a personal invitation to each of us and has a totally practical application!

During the sovereign visitation of glory we described earlier, our church congregation went on a corporate twenty-one day fast and the Holy Spirit came down in power. I (Bonnie) was praying one of those days and I fell into a trance. Before me rose a wide regal stair and I knew the Father was enthroned at the top. I was humbly bowed at the bottom, making my petitions, quoting Scriptures, and presenting myself according to our usual Charismatic traditions. I remember quoting this verse in my mind: *"Let us therefore, come boldly to the throne of grace, that we may attain mercy and find grace to help in time of need"* (Heb. 4:16). To my right was an altar of fire, and when I saw it, I also was aware of the Presence of the Son and the Holy Spirit. But in relation to my "boldness," they were positioned more deferentially to the Father than to me. I quickly moved back until I was sure they were present between me and ascendance to God's face.

I had assumed that I knew the way to approach the Father in prayer. Yet, I seemed to hear God say to me gently, "You've come up the wrong way." I replied, "Lord, help me understand." Suddenly the scene changed. I was in the midst of a jostling crowd in ancient Jerusalem. I looked up to see the form of the top of the cross going by on the road! I pushed my way through the crowd and fell into the path where Jesus was. I cried, "Lord, what can I do? What can I do?" I was offering to carry His cross or help Him carry it. He was already so abused. With eyes of love He looked at me and saw me through and through. Then He turned to continue on. He took a few steps and seemed to pass beyond a barrier through which I could dimly see. I ran to catch Him, thinking to burst through the barrier, but it completely repelled me. I could not break through to go with Him. I could only watch as He ascended the hill to be crucified.

Again I cried, "Lord, what can I do? What can I do?" In answer, I immediately heard the voice of the Father from His high place. He said, "Bonnie, you need to get to know the blood that has redeemed you." I suddenly understood there was much about Calvary I really didn't understand. And while receiving it all by faith was enough to completely save me, the depth of its truth was missing in my personal knowledge. He was calling me to an intimate personal relationship with the cross beyond my understanding then. I knew it would have a significant impact on my daily relationship with Him.

We all need to get to know the power and the glory of the blood that has redeemed us. We see through a glass dimly now, but the spirit world knows exactly what has happened. It has been subjected to the King of Glory and those who bear His name in the shadow of the cross. From Adam's day until now, the blood is a voice that silences every argument and vanquishes every opposing force. The cross is the victory won. The resurrection endorses, proclaims, and demonstrates that victory. So we see the immutable bond between the cross and the glory.

> *Behold, My Servant shall deal prudently; He shall be exalted and extolled and be very high. Just as many were astonished at you, so His visage was marred more than any man, and His form more than the sons of men; So shall He sprinkle many nations. Kings shall shut their mouths at Him; for what had not been told them they shall see, and what they had not heard they shall consider* (Isaiah 52:13-15).

Through His suffering as a seeming victim, Christ becomes the Victor. That explains human suffering as far as it can be explained. It's the great mystery of the cross. The cross challenges our view of life and our fear of death. It demands a review of how we approach life in this world and anticipate life in the world to come. This is the glory of the cross. We will still be discovering its glory for all eternity.

RADIANT FROM WITHIN

On the day of Christ's appearing, we will be fully united with Him in glory. Actually, we will all be exactly like Him in every single way. The ecstasy we will experience will leave every earthly shadow lying forgotten behind us like disappearing dust.

The cross is our access to the glory. The power is present and is working in our lives hour by hour. Its blood provides fellowship and continually draws us into personal intimacy with God. The blood speaks with a voice of authority. It is the blood of the Glorious One. It shouts down all other voices. Christ gives His glory to those who are washed in His blood. This glory is costly. It was paid for at Calvary.

If we perceive the glory of God as an impersonal phenomenon or as a thing instead of the Person, we miss it. When we cry, "Lord, we want to see Your glory!" we must be ready to receive Him as He is. John said, *"And the Word became flesh and dwelt among us, and we beheld His glory, the glory as of the only begotten of the Father, full of grace and truth"* (John 1:14). The essence of Father, Son, and Spirit, is Servant one to the other—and even Servant to the object of His affection, the Church. The day Jesus died was a new beginning. The cross is the intersection where Heaven meets earth. Under its shadow a little flock gathers and His glory shines down on those sheep in radiant, loving beams. He sends His glorious Spirit to seal our salvation and bring forth Himself in us. As we grow in faith and freedom, He begins to shine in us from the inside out. In all this powerful working, He is the gentlest Person we could know. He saturates our hearts with assurance so that we receive a deposit of the knowledge that truly all is well.

Elijah was a man just like us. He experienced God's presence in power but in Elijah's darkest hour the Lord came as a still small voice to coax him out of despair and stand Elijah on his feet in his calling.

The prophet had run to the wilderness and was living in a cave. There the word of the Lord came and said, "What are you doing here, Elijah?"

Elijah replied, "Oh Lord, I've been so zealous for You and everyone else around me has completely forsaken You. They are even after my life. What kind of payment is that?"

But the Lord said, "Come here. Let Me show you something." And He took Elijah by the hand.

As they stood at the mouth of the cave, the Lord passed by. A wind tore the mountain. Rocks were flying everywhere. But the Presence was not in the wind. Next an earthquake rumbled. The ground moved under the prophet's feet, but the Lord was not in the earthquake. Then there came a raging fire, but the Lord was not in the terrible flames. And after all this, Elijah heard it, the sound of a soft, low whisper. He wrapped his face in his cloak and ventured into the light. Then a voice told him clearly, "It's time to get on with My mission" (see 1 Kings 19:9-13).

The Spirit freshly anointed the servant and showed him an unfolding-glory-story in which Elijah played a most important part. The same Spirit that came on Elijah is the Spirit of the Lord in you. You have an anointing. Come out of your cave and use it. The anointing that is in you is the same pillar of fire and cloud of glory that rested on the ark of Israel. They saw Him clearly day after day. His glory is working in those of us who know Him. We are participators with Him now.

A thousand suns of love, hope, and healing broke through every wound Christ bore in His body, and He invites us into that fellowship to partake of His suffering until the glory of His resurrection is seen rising upon us. From inside out He is revealing His glory, and we find ourselves singing, "Holy, holy holy!" Let us draw Him more fully into our hearts and into our every day lives until we become a temple so filled with His presence that He radiates out through us in love.

ENDNOTES

1. From *The Dream of the Rood,* lines 14-20, 21-23. Translation copyright © 1982, Jonathan A. Glenn. Used by permission.

2. Matt. 26:12; Mark 14:8; John 12:7.

3. See "halal"; http://www.studylight.org/lex/heb/view.cgi ?number=01984.

4. When Ben was three months old and in the hospital, we saw the glory of the Lord come around him in a miraculous way, and the Lord completely healed him, healing his kidneys and his whole urinary system. A few years later, we stepped into a living experience of Exodus 23:25-26, which reads, *"you shall serve the Lord your God, and He will bless your bread and your water. And I will take sickness away from the midst of you....I will fulfill the number of your days."* God led us to those verses when Ben had become deathly sick again and could not keep anything down, not even water. After leading Ben to say, "God is blessing my water and my bread, and He's taking sickness away from my midst," the Holy Spirit came over him and his color came back. That time, his healing was complete.

5. See "kabowd"; http://www.studylight.org/lex/heb/view.cgi ?number=03519.

6. See "emanant"; http://machaut.uchicago.edu/?resource =Webster's&word=emanant&use1913=on.

CHAPTER 3

EPICENTER OF GLORY

I was hewn at holt's end,
moved from my stem. Strong fiends seized me there,
worked me for spectacle; cursèd ones lifted me.
On shoulders men bore me there, then fixed me on hill;
fiends enough fastened me. Then saw I mankind's Lord
come with great courage when he would mount on me.
Then dared I not against the Lord's word
bend or break, when I saw earth's
fields shake. All fiends
I could have felled, but I stood fast.[1]

My brother and Cephas came running. It was already expected that we would be betrothed, Cephas and I. He was more like a second brother than anything else in those days. The two of them, he and my brother John, were relentless teasers whenever mother and father were not within hearing. Their heads came into view in the doorway, wide eyed and excited.

"A king! A king is coming!" John said, breathless.

"He's riding on a donkey!" Cephas added.

They were out the door as quickly as they had appeared.

Mother looked up from where she kneaded the dough of our bread for the morrow. In a few days there would be no leaven in our bread or in our house. It was approaching Passover, and the inns were already filling up. Every neighbor had overflowing houses as family came in from the surrounding country to keep the Feast. Festive preparations had begun in every home. We hurried to finish and join our neighbors turning out in time to see the High Priest leading the national lamb toward the Temple square.

Mother stood, wiping her hands on her apron. Before she could say not to, I was out the door after the boys.

"Who is He?" I shouted.

Waving palms and strains of singing were everywhere. People came running from every doorway and every alley. The feeling of our first deliverance from Pharaoh was in the air, the memorial of the birth-night of our nation. The whole land yearned to throw off the bonds of our Roman occupiers. We placed our hope on the innocent sacrifice the High Priest drew along behind him in the parade.

"Hosanna! Blessed is He who comes!"

I could just see the top of the Priest's crown processing beyond our neighbors' heads. The people along the parade route regaled him with ceremonial shouting. I couldn't see his expression, but I thought it must be something to have the whole city turn out to receive you.

"O Lord, save! O Lord, send prosperity!"

The Pesach processional came down from Olivet and marched toward the East Gate. I got on hands and knees and pushed my way through the legs of the onlookers. The advantage a child has! Just beyond the ankles of my neighbors I saw the hooves of our national sacrifice tripping along behind the High Priest. He passed by with the lamb in tow. It would be put on display until the slaughter as Moses commanded. A perfect lamb without spot or blemish.

"Blessed is He who comes in the name of the Lord!"

At the moment the priest and our lamb passed under the arch of the entrance to the Temple Mount, the crowd's attention turned. Now we all strained to see *Him* coming into the city in the wake. I imagined even the priest knew by now the rumors of the Nazarene that swept the countryside, everyone wondering if He would make himself known at Pesach. He rode a donkey's colt just as they had said. More people came out of their houses to see Him, their faces inquiring, uncertain at first. It was mostly the children who were caught up in the fervor.

"Ouch! Stop pushing!"

"You stepped on my foot!"

Jostling and jockeying for position, everyone was trying to get in front of everyone else.

"Where is He from?" someone asked.

"Is this Him...*the one prophesied?"*

The river of excitement burst over its banks. The crowd swelled, a shout went up and excited folk tumbled into the road. There before us, a group of His own surrounding Him, He rode toward the city gate.

"Galileans from the look of them," someone muttered.

Another pointed.

"There! There He is!"

"Hosanna!" someone else exclaimed. Then mayhem broke out.

"Lord, save us! Hosanna!"

People began to pull off their outer garments and throw them into the road. I managed to stand up as the party came down toward us. The throng parted, and I saw Him. There, in their midst, was this king my brother had announced. He was very ordinary looking, and I suppose that surprised me the most. I don't know what we had expected.

"It's the Nazarene!"

"Tell the daughter of Zion, your king comes to you, sitting on a donkey's colt." The voice at my ear was full and breathless, half wonder, half praise. It was my mother at my side.

Her hand went around my waist, and I shivered, not from fear or worry, but in that way I would always feel a mysterious something drawing me toward the certainty of unseen angels and glories when the strains of the shofar could be heard coming from the Temple Mount to announce the beginning of the High Holy Days.

I tucked myself against her warmth, and it seemed that she and I were one together in that moment under the bright, dry sun on the road leading into Jerusalem.

I had heard her speak of Him until my father tired of her retelling the rumors of His unusual acts. Marvelous things that included even the dead being brought to life again. At least it was what the women at the well gossiped about whenever we went to draw water for our household. But not everyone believed Him. In the end Father forbade her to speak of Him anymore.

"Can anything good come out of Nazareth?" he would say.

I looked up at her.

"Hosanna!" the throng shouted in unison.

A tear of hope ran down her face.

"Will He now restore the kingdom, mother?" I whispered.

"Hosanna! Blessed is He who comes in the name of the Lord!" the crowd shouted.

She did not answer me, but began to join with the throng, her voice rising in jubilation. She seemed transfixed, and I suppose it was a good thing, for out of nowhere Cephas suddenly appeared before me, his face bright with excitement, and he kissed me.

"I shall marry you!" he announced. *"Bride and bridegroom!"* And then he laughed. He pressed something into my palm and was gone into the crowd. I flushed with fear of being seen kissed like that. I looked down and I opened my hand. A tiny

wooden lamb, artfully carved as I knew Cephas was apt to do, lay nestled in the fold of my palm.

A bride to be, I thought, *perfect, without spot or blemish.*

The man on the donkey drew nearer. Hosannas went up all around me.

"Blessed is He who comes!" the throng shouted over and over. Everyone was like an excited child now. In another moment my voice was raised with Mother's and the rest. She and I clung tightly to each other. We seemed a symbol of our whole heritage and family name, arms about one another's waists, acknowledging the son of David as He rode into our holy city. My hand tight around Cephas' promise, I lay the lamb upon my heart.

† † † † † † † † † † † †

Glory is distinguished by the source to which it is specifically related. There are different kinds of glory. The glory of God is one kind of glory. The glory of the kingdoms of this world are expressions of their own. The glory of His Kingdom is related to and flows from His personal glory. When God confers His glory upon His people, His Church, and Israel, it is no small thing.

He said, "I will not give My glory to another" (see Isa. 42:8). And yet God *is* willing to share His glory with those He brings forth in His image and likeness. He bestows His glory on those who share in Him. He makes them glory bearers. He does this by His Spirit. He bore the cross to bestow His glory on us.

The Father first conferred this glory explicitly and fully upon His Son because of the love expressed in the communion of the Godhead. By sharing His glory with Jesus, He communicated a particular intention to accomplish a mission. Jesus prayed, *"Father, the hour has come; glorify Your Son, that the Son may glorify You..."'* (John 17:1 NASB). A particular, preplanned event embodied His mission to earth. He called it the hour for which He came. That hour glorified the Father and the Son. It was the hour of God's glory revealed in multi-faceted splendor as seen in Jesus' High Priestly prayer.

A primary facet of His glory is the glory of God's authority:

> *...even as You gave Him authority over all flesh, that to all whom You have given Him, He may give eternal life. This is eternal life, that they may know You, the only true God, and Jesus Christ whom You have sent* (John 17:2-3 NASB).

Glory is God Himself revealed and shown plainly as He is. The next verse reads, *"I glorified You on the earth, having accomplished the work which You have given Me to do"* (John 17:4 NASB).

Glory is the communion of the Godhead:

> *Now, Father, glorify Me together with Yourself, with the glory which I had with You before the world was. I have manifested Your name to the men whom You gave Me out of the world; they were Yours and You gave them to Me, and they have kept Your word. Now they have come to know that everything You have given Me is from You* (John 17:5-7 NASB).

Glory is understood as issuing from within and as shining from without. It is power and honor and wealth (see Rev. 5:11-12).

Glory is unity in His creation through harmony with His Word, conveyed from Him to those who obey:

...for the words which You gave Me I have given to them; and they received them and truly understood that I came forth from You, and they believed that You sent Me. I ask on their behalf; I do not ask on behalf of the world, but of those whom You have given Me; for they are Yours; and all things that are Mine are Yours, and Yours are Mine; and I have been glorified in them (John 17:8-10 NASB).

The glory of God remains on the earth in the Church: The Church is a faithful wife to her husband Jesus and does not share herself in intimate communion with any other.

I am no longer in the world; and yet they themselves are in the world, and I come to You Holy Father, keep them in Your name, the name which You have given Me, that they may be one even as We are (John 17:11 NASB).

Glory is in pure fellowship:

While I was with them, I was keeping them in Your name which You have given Me; and I guarded them and not one of them perished but the son of perdition, so that the Scripture would be fulfilled (John 17:12 NASB).

Glory is in the Word, and it sanctifies His disciples:

But now I come to You; and these things I speak in the world so that they may have My joy made full in them-selves. I have given them Your word; and the world has hated them, because they are not of the world, even as I am not of the world. I do not ask You to take them out of the world, but to keep them from the evil one. They are not of the world, even as I am not of the world. Sanctify them in the truth; Your word is truth. As You sent Me into the world, I also have sent them into the world. For their sakes I sanctify Myself, that they themselves also may be sanctified in truth. I do not ask on behalf of these alone, but for those also who believe in Me through their word (John 17:13-20 NASB).

God's glory brings His body into oneness with Himself:

...that they may all be one; even as You, Father, are in Me and I in You, that they also may be in Us, so that the world may believe that You sent Me (John 17:21 NASB).

This oneness is the intimacy of "knowing" as a man knows his wife in married, physical union. The two become counterparts of one another, integrated, complementary, fulfilling one another. They become one. Likewise the glory of God is in His Church.

Glory is shared with those who are one with Him in love, obedience, and purpose:

The glory which You have given Me I have given to them, that they may be one, just as We are one; I in them and You in Me, that they may be perfected in unity... (John 17:22-23 NASB).

Glory is observable. The verse above continues, *"...so that the world may know that You sent Me, and loved them, even as You have loved Me"* (John 17:23 NASB). The knowledge of glory is ultimately the revelation of the Gospel.

The glory of God is the recognized demonstration of His divine attributes at work. When referring to glory, the Gospels and the apostles' writings couple it with eternal reward—and the frightful awe experienced toward God as a result of Him revealing Himself. Human glory, the glory of the kingdoms of this world, the glory of created things, is transitory and the opposite of the glory of God. The glory of God's Kingdom is spoken of as existing and active eternally.

The glory of God is revealed. His glory is sacred, private, intimate, and eternal. The glory is to be entered into and shared by all who know Him. Jesus said we will see, experience, and participate in His glory. His glory creates unity among them. His glory unites us with the Father and with Christ Himself. The glory causes the mighty seraphim serving at God's throne to cry out "Holy!" continually. Every time they turn, they see a new facet of His majesty revealed.

His glory is coming:

> *Father, I desire that they also, whom You have given Me, be with Me where I am, so that they may see My glory which You have given Me, for You loved Me before the foundation of the world. O righteous Father, although the world has not known You, yet I have known You; and these have known that You sent Me* (John 17:24-25 NASB).

His glory is summed up as the demonstration of His love:

...and I have made Your name known to them, and will make it known, so that the love with which You loved Me may be in them, and I in them (John 17:26 NASB).

BOUND TO BE LOOSED

Like the tree that Moses felled to treat the bitter pool in the wilderness, the glory of the cross is the power to heal. We understand miracles as an overflow, a demonstration of the Kingdom of the Christ. God's miracles and the outshining of His manifest Presence are conceived in the womb of the cross and issue forth from His majesty, revealed as the sacrificed Lamb.

Augustine tells of a woman, Innocentia, of "highest rank in the state." She was stricken with breast cancer, and having been told by physicians that her condition was incurable, entrusted herself to God and prayer. As Easter approached, Innocentia had a dream in which she was told to wait at the baptistry for the first woman who would come out after being baptized, and to ask this woman to make the sign of the cross over her cancerous breast. Innocentia did as she was told, and she was completely cured. Augustine wrote:

> I was indignant that so astounding a miracle, performed in so important a city, and on a person far from obscure, should have been kept a secret like this; and I thought it right to admonish her and to speak to her with some sharpness on the matter... What do these miracles attest but the faith which proclaims that Christ rose in the flesh and ascended into heaven with the flesh?...God may himself perform them by himself, through that wonderful operation of his power whereby, being eternal, he is active

> in temporal events; or he may effect them through the agency of his servants.... Be that as it may, they all testify to the faith in which the resurrection to eternal life is proclaimed.[2]

The glory rests on the testimony of what the Lord has done. Every testimony is pregnant with life for innumerable miracles. Many years ago, my friend, Jim Croft, and I (Mahesh) were ministering together in Missouri. We were young pastors who had learned much from assisting our mentor, Derek Prince, and the Lord was releasing us in the ministry of deliverance. We had a lot of zeal and were learning wisdom from the Lord.

One evening we ministered to a beautiful young lady who was ravaged by drugs. Her addictions had opened her to heavy demonic oppression, and she had come for deliverance. When the demons came to the surface, the woman began to manifest violently, and six men could not restrain her. This young girl was literally throwing them across the church. Then, as we prayed, she began to meow like a cat—it was eerie and made our hair stand on end. For hours, Jim and I were truly wrestling with unseen dark forces. The manifestations would subside and then surge again. Late into the night we finished praying for her, but with no conclusion.

The following morning we had another meeting. As we worshiped, the whole congregation entered into praise, and the sweet Spirit descended and enveloped all of us in His presence. Suddenly, we heard the most beautiful song of the Spirit coming from the back of the church. I looked, and it was the young oppressed girl from the night before. In that wonderful atmosphere of worship, the glory had descended. The girl had stepped into a bubble of His presence. In that moment, simply in worship, God completely delivered her, cleansing her instantly by the blood of the Lamb.

What happened? The power of the cross was active and demonstrated in the glory. The cross and the glory are inextricably united. Throughout both the Old and New Testaments, we can see it. The glory on Sinai was revealed *after* and made possible *because* the Passover lamb had been slain. This blood and His glory accompany each other. Where the blood of the Lamb is demonstrated, the glory will be manifest. Where the glory of God is manifest the blood of the Lamb will be demonstrated. We pray, "Show us Your glory!" As we bear the image of the Son in His death, we will bear the image of His glory. Throughout the history of the Tabernacle and Temple, the glory and the sacrificial blood were present together. Yet when the sacrifices were reduced to religious routines, the glory lifted. The divine convergence of God's bloody sacrifice and His glory cannot be separated any more than He can be separated from Himself.

John the Baptist saw the Holy Spirit descend on Jesus: *"I saw the Spirit descending from heaven like a dove, and He remained upon Him"* (John 1:32). *Seeing Him, John knew the Son as the Lamb. He is "the Lamb slain from the foundation of the world"* (Rev. 13:8). Before God ever created humans for fellowship with Him, He devised the plan that would secure access for that communion with Him. The blood makes the way.

Bound in human flesh, Christ was carried to the cross. There He displayed His glory and set loose the power of His exchange in all who surrender to His Lordship. In perfect self-giving He continues, from throne to cross, cross to throne, and from the throne the outpoured Life-giving Spirit.

THE FINISHED WORK

The finished work of the cross provides perfectly perfect redemption through the seven-fold shedding of the blood of Jesus. The High Priest would make atonement once a year by seven-fold sprinkling of blood in the Holy of Holies. Jesus sprinkled His blood in agony in the Garden; from His face when they plucked out His beard; from His back when they beat Him with rods; from His brow when they pressed a crown of thorns into it; from His back when they lashed Him with a whip; from His hands and His feet when they nailed Him to the tree; and from His side when a soldier pierced Him with a spear. The blood effectively ministers its effectiveness to those who believe. It "speaks" hour by hour (see Heb. 12:24).

With His last breath and last drop of blood, Jesus made seven exclamations from the cross. The first is the word of forgiveness for His enemies: *"Then Jesus said, "Father forgive them, for they know not what they do"* (Luke 23:24). As He made intercession for them, they hurled abuses and fought over who got His clothing.

The second word is the promise of eternal life, His life in exchange for yours and mine. *"And Jesus said to him, 'Assuredly, I say to you today you shall be with Me in paradise'"* (Luke 23:43).

The third word is to His family:

> *Now there stood by the cross of Jesus His mother, and His mother's sister, Mary the wife of Clopas, and Mary Magdalene. When Jesus therefore saw His mother, and the disciple whom He loved standing by, He said to His mother, "Woman, behold your son!" Then He said to the disciple, "Behold your mother!"* (John 19:25-27)

In the hour of His greatest torture, He thought first of the people who loved Him, His mother and John.

The fourth word is addressed to God by the Man when He is rejected as sin: *"My God, My God, why have You forsaken Me?"* (Matt. 27:46; Mark 15:34). We remember these words whenever it seems He is far from our situation.

The fifth word is: *"I thirst."* It is spoken, *"...that the Scripture might be fulfilled"* (John 18:28). He turned water to wine and had command of Heaven's host, but He filled the cup of salvation with His own blood and said, "Let all who are thirsty come and drink" (see John 7:37).

His sixth word is, *"It is finished!"* (John 19:30). This was not the cry of a vanquished victim. It was the Victor's declaration that the work He came to do was accomplished. He had completed His mission.

The seventh word from the cross is a prayer: *"Father, into Your hands I commit My Spirit"* (Luke 23:46). This prayer is the last utterance made by a devout Jew before He lays down to sleep at night. It shows us Jesus' perfect trust in His Father to raise Him up "in the morning" and deliver Him from the grave.

In these seven words from the cross, Jesus addresses every human dilemma. He speaks to every person and draws them into love's embrace.

> *But God forbid that I should boast except in the cross of our Lord Jesus Christ, by whom the world has been crucified to me, and I to the world* (Galatians 6:14).

COSMIC SPECTACLE

In the cosmic spectacle that shocked the natural world and turned the spirit world on its ear, Jesus won the greatest battle in history—the battle to redeem men's souls from darkness. In the shadow of the cross we see full light. In the cross we see God in all of His glory. But how can that be? Death on a cross was the cruelest form of execution. Death on a cross was reserved for the lowest criminal element, traitors, murderers, and such. Yet, it was the death of a Servant who took on Himself the offenses of the whole world from before, during, and even after His sufferings, that bespeaks the ultimate glory. Jesus said:

> *The hour has come that the Son of Man should be glo-*
> *rified. Most assuredly, I say to you, unless a grain of*
> *wheat falls into the ground and dies, it remains alone;*
> *but if it dies, it produces much grain. He who loves his*
> *life will lose it, and he who hates his life in this world*
> *will keep it for eternal life. If anyone serves Me, let him*
> *follow Me; and where I am, there My servant will be*
> *also. If anyone serves Me, him My Father will honor*
> (John 12:23-27).

Humanly speaking, the thought of suffering and death is repulsive. Jesus agonized in Gethsemane and submitted Himself to death on the cross. Life for the world was born through His suffering. The suffering of Christ began in the womb of the virgin. He took off His garment of glory and clothed Himself in the weakness as an ordinary human. He was disbelieved, accused, abused, and rejected by His own community. He constantly experienced men's distance from God and it grieved Him day after day. He went hungry and thirsty, was weary and without a home of His own to settle down in. His suffering made way for His glory. The cross gives us a glimpse into glory that is otherwise utterly hidden from our natural understanding.

TIME FOR GLORY

Before you ever prayed your first prayer, uttered your first cry at injustice, felt your first longing for God, felt your first sigh of despair, He already answered. God heard you at Calvary and He answered you completely there. All your losses were compensated there. Consolation for every injury of body and mind is in Him there. Provision for every loss and healing for all disease is unleashed in His body on the Tree. There is justice, there is liberation; relief from torment is there. There is wonder-working power in His blood. That power is the glory of the Father as He abides in us to minister by His Holy Spirit. The Comforter has come. He descends upon the Lamb and fills the empty place. *"Before they call I will answer; while they are yet speaking I will hear"* (Isa. 65:24).

Human injustice and suffering, oppression, and disease are all evidence that we live in an imperfect world.

> *For the creation was subjected to futility, not willingly, but because of Him who subjected it in hope; because the creation itself also will be delivered from the bondage of corruption into the glorious liberty of the children of God* (Romans 8:20-21).

But now the blood answers and God creates all things new. Our perfect Father has made the way for the return of His glory. His Spirit comes to renew the face of the earth. The blood of Christ is fresh and living. It builds the bridge between the imperfections of this realm and the Perfection of Heaven. The blood speaks. It answers the heart cry of your soul and brings you to His glorious liberty. The power of resurrection is unleashed and we are out of our graves. The blood goes before us and we come along the ruddy road following in the footsteps of the Crucified who loves us and gave Himself so that we might find our way to where He is. The blood comes along, cleaning up behind us and leaving no trace of anything but glory. The mystery of miracles is the dual enfolding by the blood and of the Spirit. This is the gift of the children of God. With Him nothing is too difficult. No future is too bleak, no failure too far, no vengeance too strong, no suffering too great, no violence too brutal, that He cannot prevail for you. And He does. This is the time for glory.

A mother brought her daughter to us. The daughter had been physically and sexually brutalized, and almost murdered. The violent abuse that young woman had experienced could have shattered her irrevocably in mind and body. When she came for prayer during a conference gathering, we felt great compassion. We were humbled to see her courage. I (Mahesh) did not minister to her right away. I was waiting until I sensed the glory of the Healer. Jesus is the Re-creator. When He does His work, He can finish it in an instant.

As I sensed Him present to heal, I called the young woman to me. As we prayed, I was aware that the Mender of Hearts arose. Jesus the Mediator stood between us. He stood between her and everything else. Between her and everyone else, including the man who had done these terrible things to her. Christ was between her and her pain, between her and the violence, between her and the memory of her trauma, between her and all that had happened, between her and the past and its shattered future. Christ stood in those broken-down places and began building up the gap in her wall. Her countenance changed. The shadow moved from over her heart. As His light began to shine from inside out, it was but a few moments before joy filled her heart!

Within a week she contacted us again. We gloried as we heard her rejoice, "This week has been the best week of my entire life!" Before the young woman called, Christ had answered from Calvary. "It is finished!" He had told her. This is the testimony of power in the cross that releases the Spirit to heal what is broken and resurrect the dead. It's only a glimpse of the majesty on display for His Bride. Before we call, God answers in His Son. Step into Him more fully today. His provision is as glorious as it is precious. And it is as precious as it is made fresh by His blood. He makes us the partakers. He makes us whole. He makes us His healers.

NATURAL AVERSION

Each of us possesses a natural aversion to what the scenes of Calvary would parade before us. Like the disciples on the road to Emmaus, we are full of questions and slow to believe that such seeming defeat could result in victory. And yet, when He opens our eyes, we recognize Him and suddenly we "get it."

> *"O foolish ones, and slow of heart to believe in all that the prophets have spoken! Ought not the Christ to have suffered these things and to enter into His glory?" And beginning at Moses and all the Prophets, He expounded to them in all the Scriptures the things concerning Himself* (Luke 24:25-27).

We read in Ephesians chapter 2 that the cross has brought us to the Father, through the Son, by the Spirit. It was not the Son only at the cross. The Father was there, fully engaged and giving all of Himself in love. The Son offered Himself up fully and willingly. And He did so through the Holy Spirit. Hebrews 9:14 says that Jesus, *"...through the eternal Spirit offered Himself without spot to God."* We tend to imagine an Individual Person, Jesus, suffering for the sin of the world when we think of Calvary. But Father and Spirit were there too, completely involved, totally giving and forgiving us all.

The Holy Spirit manifests the intense emotions, of the Godhead. Far from being an impersonal elemental force, He is power and Person. He embodies love as described in First Corinthians chapter 13. He is love that bears, hopes, and believes all things, endures all things. He never fails.

As we experience the fresh advent of revival, we are rediscovering the passion, costliness, and depth of God's love. His love dominates every aspect of His eternal nature. Love is the only source of true freedom. True love sets people free. Free from sin. Free from guilt. Free from fear. Love said, *"I came that they may have life and have it abundantly"* (John 10:10 ESV).

In 1410, Andrei Rublev painted a masterful icon picturing the Trinity. In it Father, Son, and Spirit sit around a table on which stands a cup filled with blood. Each One is fully engaged and deferring to the Other. They are constructing the masterful plan to recover the human race. Seated between Father and Spirit, the Son rests two fingers on the table near the cup. As His eyes look lovingly to the Father, one might almost hear Him say, "I'll go down and do it." The Spirit looks toward the Son as if to say, "I'll go with You." The Passion of Christ was pre-planned. The Father was fully giving the Son; the Son was fully offering Himself, and the Holy Spirit was fully indwelling and enabling the will of the Father through the Son. Heaven was opened to the citizens of earth.

We have access to the Father through the Son by the Spirit. It's active fellowship. Our access means we have been brought face to face, invited into the glorious realm of the Godhead to sit at the table with Him in conversation, in communion, in the very fellowship and counsel of God Almighty. The cross opens the door. The Spirit forges the bond. The blood and the glorious Presence are one.

The death of Jesus was not the interruption of His life, but rather its ultimate purpose. The early Church writers move from His birth to His death in a single breath, having realized that the entire purpose of His life in the flesh was for death. That is exactly what the Savior said time and again to His followers, although they found it hard to hear. Dullness toward the cross pervades the human mind-set.

Yet as we embrace His cross, we experience His glorious victory:

For I consider that the sufferings of this present time are not worthy to be compared with the glory which shall be revealed in us. For the earnest expectation of the creation eagerly waits for the revealing of the sons of God. For the creation was subjected to futility, not willingly, but because of Him who subjected it in hope; because the creation itself also will be delivered from the bondage of corruption into the glorious liberty of the children of God. For we know that the whole creation groans and labors with birth pangs together until now (Romans 8:18-22).

All creation is waiting for something. It's waiting for the manifestation of the sons of God. We pray,

that I may know Him and the power of His resurrection, and the fellowship of His sufferings, being conformed to His death, if, by any means, I may attain to the resurrection from the dead (Philippians 3:10-11).

THE ETERNAL CONFESSION

Mahesh and I were ministering in California when Mahesh had a word of knowledge about a child that was suffering from an eye disorder called nystagmus. Two of our children were born with this congenital birth defect of involuntary movement of the eyes, so when Mahesh gave this word, my human empathy and compassion reached out to this family. I found myself standing up and looking over the crowd to see who responded. A mother with her young daughter in her arms immediately stood up. Mahesh released a word of healing, and then continued to minister. We found out later that the little girl's vision problem was so serious that she could barely see. But after Mahesh prayed, the mother reported that her little girl pointed to me and asked her mother, "Mommy, who is that woman standing there that is covered in blood?" I had just been ministering on the power of the Blood of Jesus. She was not frightened. She got a revelation. She was seeing spiritual realities as her natural eyes were touched. She was seeing the reality of the living Christ available to us through the shed blood of Calvary.

> *Surely He has borne our griefs and carried our sorrows....*
> *He was wounded for our transgressions, He was bruised*
> *for our iniquities...and by His stripes we are healed* (Isaiah
> 53:4-5).

The Lamb was slain once, but that single event is our eternal confession. It propels us from grace to grace, from glory to glory. Our confession and surrender bring us an anointing. Glory comes into our lives. This mystery is affecting you, capturing you, and making you someone who is going to live forever in the company of Jesus Christ. The Lord is awakening us. We are coming to the epicenter of glory. At Calvary we are transfused, His blood for our life. From Calvary to Pentecost, which is the Father's promise of the Spirit. He has come. He is in you. The shout of Calvary resounds on the wings of the Spirit. A voice cries out "Glory!" *"Let God arise, let His enemies be scattered"* (Ps. 68:1).

ENDNOTES

1. From *The Dream of the Rood,* lines 29-38. Translation copyright © 1982, Jonathan A. Glenn. Used by permission.

2. Augustine of Hippo, *The City of God,* trans. Marcus Dods, D.D. (New York, NY: Hafner Publishing Company, 1948), 488, 491.

CHAPTER 4

BRINGING MANY SONS TO GLORY

Now you may know, loved man of mine,
what I, work of baleful ones, have endured
of sore sorrows. Now has the time come
when they will honor me far and wide,
men over earth, and all this great creation,
will pray for themselves to this beacon. On me God's son
suffered awhile. Therefore I, glorious now,
rise under heaven, and I may heal
any of those who will reverence me.[1]

✝ ✝ ✝ ✝ ✝ ✝ ✝ ✝ ✝ ✝ ✝ ✝ ✝

One could hear the sound of their voices before they reached the watchtower. The boy there was dozing as usual. The rise and fall of the interchange and laughter between friends was soft on the night air. Their voices were familiar to me for they often came whenever they were in Judea. They would meet to sit and talk beneath my branches and then go up to the Mount for prayers.

His conversations were different from most. He addressed the Holy One as "My Father" in a way that made me know that it was true. Though the Father He spoke to never showed Himself, I was sure He was there that night somewhere just beyond the shadows cast by the moon through my thick foliage.

There had been a stir about Nazarene. He was accustomed to keeping watch among us in the garden—Gethsemane, the oil press. Sometimes He would crouch in my shade, leaning His back against my side as a sigh escaped Him, as if He carried the weight of the world and there was no one to support Him. I lent Him such strength as I could, but I never saw Him before or after like He was on the last night He came.

He paced and seemed agitated, sometimes wringing His hands. He even rebuked those friends who came with Him, but only once.

"Could you not even keep watch with me one hour?"

They seemed ashamed. They had all been feasting. They roused up for a little while before the effects of their wine and supper outran their best intentions and they drifted off again. Their heavy breathing mixed with the night air.

It was Pesach. Passover, the night of the lamb. In the distance a cur howled as it roamed about under the cover of dark alleys in search of some reward. The rest of the city was filled with the sound of the Feast. Reminiscence hung on the atmosphere. Jerusalem picked up her glittering skirts and tripped backward in time. She was gathering her children as a hen her chicks. She bore them back, retelling the great deliverance. That night they all remembered. Around every Pesach meal they were resettled for a moment along the banks of the Nile in Egypt, the old fathers repeating to their children what the Lord had done. They were in Goshen. And while Egypt fumbled in darkness, Israel had light.

The blood of the lamb freshly struck on post and lintel as midnight approached, Jacob's children prepared for Exodus. Their time of escape had come. The time of going out from bondage amidst the sounds of the cry of the firstborn of their captors.

The Man lay prostrate on His face at my feet. Once He reached out and took hold of my roots for His anchor, as if the floor of our garden were a ship tossed and I might keep Him from falling away into a great storm.

I would have held Him had I arms that could reach around Him. His friends slept. He cried out. His head was wet with passion and tears, and once, when He raised His troubled brow, I saw that He was red. Sweat drops of His own blood covered that graceful countenance. Drops of it fell on my root and soaked into the earth where I was planted.

"My Father!"

I had heard His words the many times He came here with His own before that night. Right words. Words of life. Words of promise. Word of God.

He cried out in anguish. Why could He be so troubled?

"If it be possible let this cup pass from Me!"

He was wrestling against powers, malevolent spirits that swirled about us in my garden. They pulled His strength from Him. I wonder if His slumbering friends could have helped at all. He might have been supported some, had they sat with Him sympathetically, awake.

Before, when He used to come here with His friends, He was only ever gentle and assuring. And I was witness to His wisdom. I had seen His joy. But on that night He had none. When His blood burst through in drops upon His brow, I wanted to put my branches down to lift Him up. I would have bent against nature if I could have—to give Him strength from my reserve. I would have lent Him oil for the pressing He endured. His heart was like an olive. His blood and sweat were crushed beneath the millstone. He was being pressed out, and it seemed that I was groaning, too.

I longed to wake those other men and draw them to His side. But then the angel came and strengthened Him. It was a most wondrous sight—the shining creature, strong and mighty, direct from Heaven. But gentle, bending soft and low, the shining creature came. Like a mother over her child and whispering to Him things that went down deep as other food and wine. Then earth's Warrior brightened. He sighed, and in a low voice I heard Him speak again to His Father.

"Have Your way and do with Me that for which I came."

The vanguard came with torches, swaggering and threatening Him as if He were some formidable foe. They were armed to the teeth as if coming for a thief or murderer. They were afraid.

The sleeping boy in the tower awoke and ran away without his clothes.

They didn't know which man they were looking for. But then one of His, a friend that used to come here with Him, stepped out from the midst of the armed men. The bleeding Watchman rose up from where He had been praying as His former friend came toward Him. The Watchmen took him in with clear eyes.

"Rabbi!" the betrayer exclaimed, stretching out his arms in greeting as if he had not seen Him for a while. And then he greeted Him with a kiss.

In return, the blood-sweated Man said something that I could not hear. And turning, He addressed the soldiers.

"I am He. I'm the Man."

If I'd had a voice like them I would have laughed out loud as those armed men fell down when He spoke. They were thugs, beasts of prey compared to Him. They bound His hands and took Him from the garden. And He resisted not a bit.

Then a strange silence settled over the garden after He was gone. His friends had all fled. The yellow torches danced slowly across the Kidron and up the hill to the High Priest's palace. Their light outlined His dark head and broad shoulders as the mob climbed up with Him as their prisoner.

I didn't see Him again after that. He never came to me anymore to keep His watch and pray. Sometime later, others that seemed to know Him came. They sat in huddles at my feet whispering about what had taken place. His fate had joined Him to another tree outside the city gates. There, they told one another, He had been hanged up as a traitor. And on that other Tree, they said, He died.

That was the night Heaven wept, and the earth around the garden opened, up and down the valley where the graves are. They said the Temple veil was rent in two from top to bottom. And they said the friend who came and kissed Him embraced a tree of his own doing down near the Potter's Field—the Field of Blood.

A few of us remain here in our garden now. Though bent with age, we still keep watch over the ancient city just across from the gate He once rode through in triumph. It is sealed now. But they say He will come again, riding through it like a King.

We still give our olives to the press. And our oil still gives light in darkness.

I still remember the look of Him on that last night. I still hear the sound of His praying, the night of keeping watch when He clung to me.

The night He cried, *"My Father!"*

That night His blood was sprinkled on my root.

Have you ever noticed how many times God shows up in a garden? Eden, the land of Israel itself, Gethsemane, the garden where Jesus' tomb was.

God's first promise was made in a garden on the day that Adam and Eve overstepped their boundaries and were banished forever from His garden of delights: *"I will put enmity between you and the woman, and between your seed and her Seed; He shall bruise your head, and you shall bruise His heel"* (Gen. 3:15). In their separation from God, there was a promise of victory to come through a Seed.

God's first command to Adam was to tend and guard His garden. After the Fall, that mission remained unchanged, although now the sowing and reaping would be accompanied by toil and pain. Ultimately, God sowed His Son, the Seed, into the rocky soil of the world. The Seed sown is the first among many brethren, the first-born of many sons. When we hear the Word and believe, we are transformed, and our inner man is recreated in His image. No longer corruptible by the power of sin and death, we become partakers of His Life-giving Spirit.

> *To them God willed to make known what are the riches of the glory of this mystery among the Gentiles: which is Christ in you, the hope of glory"* (Colossians 1:27).

This is our new identity as we become part of a new race, recreated through Jesus' death, burial, and resurrection. We are strengthened in our inner man through the riches of God's glory (see Eph. 3:16). The fruit of righteousness in us through Christ brings God praise and glory (see Phil. 1:11).

God has been on a mission, not merely to redeem the race of man, but to recreate it, to give it back its life. The revelation of the old covenant, the promise to Abraham, the Law and the Prophets— all of these point to the new thing that would be demonstrated and ratified in the incarnation. Jesus' mission was not to become a philo-sophical or theological icon. He did not come to "set a good example." His mission was to end the old Adamic race with its death-curse and to begin a new one.

His story is the new Genesis. The first woman was taken from the side of the first man. The Last Adam, Christ, carried the substance that would be formed into the companion eternally suitable for Him. His Church is that companion—we have been betrothed to the Second Man. Christ is the Head of a new creation: all who put their trust in Him.

HIS STORY IS OUR STORY

Once you find yourself in His story, the pathway leads you straight to Calvary. The cross gives access to glory. Sin has subjected creation to futility—the ongoing cycle that culminates when this world wears out like a garment (see Isa. 51:6). But Christ is the firstborn from the dead, and in Him you are now destined for glory!

This is that for which all creation presently waits. This is the overcoming. This is the victory. This is Christ in you, the hope of glory! We are not returning to that first garden paradise that was subjected not of its own will, but of Him who *"subjected it in hope"* of His salvation (see Rom. 8:20). The way back to a spoiled garden is barred forever. The whole of that first creation was enfolded in the cross, when the Last Adam declared "It is finished!" We meet the Second Man, the Life-giving Spirit, coming out of His grave in the garden. Mary thought He was the gardener. But then He called her name and she saw Him in His glory.

He is our Constant Gardener. From Eden to Israel's Promised Land, to the Garden of Gethsemane, and from the garden tomb on to the Paradise of God. We are not going back—we are going on. He is drawing us after Him in His triumph. He has created us as His Bride to be *"a help meet for him"* (Gen. 2:18 KJV).

When at last we see Him, Christ will say, "This is it! Finally, one like Me, for Me, to be with Me and beside Me. At last one to share My glory!" Then we shall know Him even as we are known (see 1 Cor. 13:12).

Just as the first garden was created for Adam, God shall set us in the midst of His new Garden of Delights. There we shall enter not into labor, toil, and the sweat of our brows, but into the rest of God eternally. We shall have reached our destination. We will be home at last.

POWER OF THE SPIRIT

The ancient doctrine of Christianity holds to the threefold appearing, *parousia*, of Christ. Christ came in the flesh; He comes in the Spirit; He will come in glory. One is past, one is present, and one is yet to come. He came the first time as the Lamb who takes away the sin of the world. In His earthly ministry, Christ waged war with the spiritual and physical powers of sickness and death. In this age He rules from His throne in Heaven. There He pours out His Spirit to infill and sanctify all who ask. He wages war with the powers that assault body, soul, and spirit in this world. At the end of the age, He shall come again in the clouds with His angels to set up His throne and vanquish forever His natural armies and spiritual enemies who have destroyed the world. For now, all creation groans in yearning for the sons of God to be clothed in His power and walking in demonstration of the glory of the Only Begotten.

The cross is the symbol of our union with Christ. It is the crossroads of all human and natural history. In Christ, creation groaned and died. In Christ, it was set free from bondage. The cross is the summary of the Gospel. It is the glad announcement of our redemption.

> *And I, brethren, when I came to you, did not come*
> *with excellence of speech or of wisdom declaring to you*

the testimony of God. For I determined not to know anything among you except Jesus Christ and Him crucified. I was with you in weakness, in fear, and in much trembling. And my speech and my preaching were not with persuasive words of human wisdom, but in demonstration of the Spirit and of power, that your faith should not be in the wisdom of men but in the power of God (1 Corinthians 2:1-5).

God revealed Himself as the deliverer and healer. He pronounced judgment on the depraved state of a fallen world. Then He turned right around and poured out His mercy on all who would receive:

Surely He has borne our griefs and carried our sorrows; yet we esteemed Him stricken, smitten by God, and afflicted. But He was wounded for our transgressions, He was bruised for our iniquities; the chastisement for our peace was upon Him, and by His stripes we are healed. All we like sheep have gone astray; we have turned, every one, to his own way; and the Lord has laid on Him the iniquity of us all (Isaiah 53:4-6).

The Lamb is our advocate, pleading righteousness before the Father. Jesus is carrying out His High Priestly office. The Holy Spirit has full access through the blood, to us. And we have full access to the Father and the Son through the Spirit. Your spirit, soul, and body have been brought into personal relationship. As we wait for His appearing, we dwell in vessels of flesh. Our earthly lives are lived out in the shadowland between the victory of the cross and the redemption of our bodies at Christ's coming. We are between "already" and "not yet." The glory that shines in this present darkness is the power of the Spirit in us through Him. Christ gave Himself in our stead. After He was taken up, He poured out His Spirit to be in us and with us:

> *And I will pray the Father and He will give you another Helper, that He may abide with you forever... I will not leave you orphans; I will come to you* (John 14:16,18).

There has been a divine exchange of Persons. We are wanderers in a wilderness that is passing away, but we are not alone. The blood provides the Holy Spirit ongoing access to our spirit, soul, and body. He resides in us, enduing us with power from on high. We have foretastes of what is to come when we will see Him face to face. Those glimpses of glory are His Presence when we pray. We glimpse His glory when we lay hands on the sick and they are healed. We glimpse His glory as we stand in the congregation of saints, hands and voices raised in adoration and harmony. Power flows from the throne where the Lamb is standing, The gifts of the Spirit and miracles are demonstrations on earth of the heavenly kingdom.

Every believer receives a measure of faith as a gift from God. When Jesus comes, He will expect a return on His down-payment. He has said, *"The works that I do you shall do and greater works than these because I go to My Father"* (John 14:12). The early Church believed and received. Now our day has come. The anointing for miracles in Jesus' name is increasing as His Day draws near. We are living now in the power of the Spirit to come. The nations shall come to the brightness of His rising (see Isa. 60:3). And the whole earth will be filled with the glory of the Lord (see Isa. 6:3, Hab. 2:14).

A New Thing

Jesus' disciples asked, *"Lord, teach us how to pray"* (Luke 11:1). They were saying, "Help us to understand to whom we are praying and how we should address Him." For the first time in the history of religion, Jesus revealed the primary way to relate to God: "Our Father." He didn't say, "Lord God who Created the Universe." He didn't say, "Mighty Captain of Armies." He didn't say, "Great Jehovah Rapha, our Doctor." What He said was, "Our Father."

In the world religions there are all kinds of approaches to God, all kinds of addresses to God, all kinds of understandings of God. But only one God can be known through the revelation of His only begotten Son: Our Father. You can only know the Father to the degree that you know His Son. Sonship is relational. Sonship is ongoing, unfolding intimacy. Jesus did not become the Son when He was conceived in Mary's womb. He is eternally Son of the Father. It gives us a beautiful picture of the nature of the Almighty. This interdependent community of Father, Son, and Spirit helps us to see God as love in Person.

There is a paradigm shift in the mind-set of the Church. God is making sons in His image, in relationship, interdependent, and in perfect communion. We reflect His glory as we relate to Him as sons and heirs of His Kingdom through Christ. (We say "sons" meaning heirs—all those who have been born of God.) Jesus is your elder brother. His Holy Spirit is working in you, conforming you in His image. If you embrace Him, you can overcome the world.

God is Father to the Son begotten in Him before the world was made. He is Father first. If we think of God first and foremost as Creator, our expectation will primarily rest on Him as our Provider. But the natural world was created for our sake and for God's glory. He gave us stewardship of it. We can only know Him as Father through the identity that Jesus supplies.

God wants us to begin to recognize and embrace Him as the Father to the Son. The writer of the letter to the Hebrews says it was fitting that He by whom and for whom all things exist should bring many sons to glory (see Heb. 2:10). God, who made rocks and trees, is first of all our Father. He created the heavens and the earth, but He fathers sons. He is God, but when we think of God first as our Father, it changes everything. It brings us near. Every event in our lives takes on new meaning. Our successes are for His glory, not our own; our trials prove our sonship; our suffering receives eternal purpose; our lives take on new value.

> *Therefore...let us lay aside every weight, and the sin which so easily ensnares us, and let us run with endurance the race that is set before us, looking unto Jesus, the author and finisher of our faith, who for the joy that was set before Him endured the cross, despising the shame, and has sat down at the right hand of the throne of God* (Hebrews 12:1-2).

The cross is the path to the Throne. If we remove the cross, the entire revelation of Scripture from Eden to the apocalypse becomes meaningless. We shall see the marks in His hands and side when He greets us, even the "Thomases" among us. And many will present the marks of their own suffering for His sake, offering them to the One they love who also suffered for them.

God had you in mind before He created the cosmos. You have been created with a specific destiny, an intention of God on your life. You are living in a certain place at a certain time with a certain family lineage for the purpose of bringing glory to God. The way to discover that glory is to embrace your identity as son to the Father in Heaven.

BECOMING AN HEIR

The Holy Spirit is called the "bond of love."[2] He said, "I will create you in My image and likeness, and I will dignify you by giving you the free will to decide what to do about it." Your ability to choose is an affirmation of God's confidence toward you and the love and liberty the Father invests in you. Every right choice is a little *yes* that you belong to Him. If you keep this in mind, your daily decisions either dignify you or deny that you have been made a son of the Father.

As heirs of His eternal Kingdom, we have been given stewardship where we are. He knew that you would be living right where you are now. He chose the lineage you were born in. He ordained a family, a body, a nation, and a time for you to live here on earth.

> *He has made from one blood every nation of men to dwell on all the face of the earth, and has determined their preappointed times and the boundaries of their dwellings* (Acts 17:26).

Every detail of your life was known before you were ever created in your mother's womb. God intends to make you a son. He ordained the circumstances of your life to take you from bondage to liberty, slavery to sonship.

The heir is a slave as long as he remains a child (see Gal. 4:1). A newly born infant is completely dependent. You have to carry a baby everywhere he needs to go. You have to feed a baby everything he needs. You have to run and pick a baby up when he cries. You even change a baby's dirty diaper. You walk the floor with a baby in the middle of the night. And as the baby grows, you begin to discipline and train the baby, along with giving him plenty of unconditional love. As a result, when the baby is thirty, he is no longer a baby, but a mature son or daughter.

Do you think that the heir is placed under the discipline of tutors to keep him down his whole life? Not at all. An heir remains a child as long as he is enslaved to his own passions. The time of instruction is meant to mature him. Once he is mature, the heir steps into the full inheritance that has been waiting. He is ready to assume responsibility for the Father's estate.

Sons Will Prosper

According to the Bible, the sons of Issachar were unique in that they "knew the times" (see 1 Chron. 12:32). They could discern the times, and they knew how to conduct themselves—which direction to go, how to give direction to other people, and more. God wants each of us to get a spirit like the sons of Issachar. Unlike the people who just do the religious thing, but lack direction and discernment, God wants to give us discernment and favor. He wants us to be sons.

When sons are trained, they can take over their father's business. In the same way, the sons and daughters of the heavenly Father can carry part of the burden of the Lord's heart. Jesus carried the burden of His heavenly Father. He came to reveal the Father to us, doing only what the Father told Him to do, thus proving Himself to be a real Son.

As you become secure in your position as a child of God and your heart carries the purposes of your heavenly Father, then it becomes His pleasure to give you His blessing. It is *"the Father's good pleasure to give you the Kingdom"* (Luke 12:32).

He wants you to become mature in your capacity to administer His blessings. God wants to give you His direction, His clarity, His blessing, and His favor—along with your share of the responsibilities of the Kingdom of God. First, though, He needs to grow you up.

I (Mahesh) am a duck and a goose hunter. I also hunt deer. Therefore, I know how to handle guns. But only when my sons were pretty well grown did I take them out and say, "OK now, this is how you handle a shotgun." I knew better than to let my four-year-old son shoot a shotgun; he had to grow up first.

God wants to give you mighty weapons that will pull down strongholds, but only as you mature and demonstrate responsibility. Some people want "the anointing" immediately, but God knows that would be like handing a 12-gauge shotgun to a child. Someone with the spiritual strength and understanding of a four-year-old cannot handle a stronghold-destroying weapon.

God is more willing to give you His anointing and power than you are willing to have it, and like a true Father, He will grow you up. He will exercise your spiritual senses and take you from glory to glory, from anointing to anointing. When you grow up enough to share His burdens, then you become a son or daughter of Issachar, one who understands the ways of God.

TAKING RESPONSIBILITY

The Greek word for "tested" does not mean temptation to sin. It implies the testing involved in purifying metal. It means to try or to scrutinize, in the way that assayers assess property in order to determine its value. It means "to prove." Testing bespeaks of *sons*, not children, and not slaves. Without testing we will not grow up to receive our inheritance in the Kingdom. The Bible calls it "suffering." And because He suffered testing, our elder Brother, Jesus, helps us when we are tested, too.

God's Kingdom is the Father's house. The Lord gives each of us areas of oversight and responsibility as His children. Jesus proved His Sonship through the discipline of obedience:

Therefore, it was necessary for Him to be made in every respect like us, His brothers and sisters, so that He could be our merciful and faithful High Priest before God...Since He Himself has gone through suffering and testing, He is able to help us when we are being tested (Hebrews 2:17-18 NLT).

We are trained by the Father through testing. Jesus was baptized and led out into the wilderness to be tested (see Matt. 4). The Father had something in mind. Jesus could have started His own miracle ministry at any time. But the Father set an appointed time to exalt Him after Jesus was tested. In this He demonstrates the nature of sonship into which we have been called.

As a Christian you have been recreated in the image of the Son of God. You are an eternal son-being. This would have been impossible except that the Son begotten of the Father shed His blood for you. It would have been impossible for any of us to be drawn into the Kingdom and reconciled to the Father as sons, except that the Son laid His life down for us.

But His death is not the end of His story or ours. The cross is the beginning, Pentecost is the middle, receiving the Kingdom is our destiny, and the resurrection is the climax. He left an example of how to handle trials and testing. Now, while we have life in our bodies, we are continually being crucified with Him. Our egos (our "I" part—"I want; I wish; I think; I feel") are being killed off as we surrender to the initiatives of the Father and respond by the grace of our Helper the Holy Spirit. The cross changes everything. It gives us balanced understanding of ourselves. Instead of trying to elude capture for our sins, we are putting our personal egos to death.

As sons, our own will is secondary to the will of the Father. The Son is given to the Father's pleasure and is interdependent with Him. The Father is not independent of the Son or the Son of the Father.

Without this interdependence, the Kingdom will not advance. God has determined to make Himself interdependent with you. Being a son does not mean "co-dependent," and it definitely does not mean *in*dependent. It is an ongoing relationship by which each one is continually built up, strengthened, edified—and glorified.

Your response to God as a son directly affects His relationship with the world. If the sons are not manifest, the Father is hidden as well. He reveals Himself in His human sons as He did in His Son Jesus.

A PROVEN VESSEL

Jesus did not need to be perfected. He had no sin. But He was tested as a Son. And as a Son, He was a Receiver so that He could be a Giver of all the Father had for the world.

Sons are servants even in the hard times. Entitlement brings people under the tyranny of sin. That's the mindset of a slave. Like the children of Israel, we have been delivered from Egypt and called out of bondage, called into receivership as heirs of the promise, but many are dying off in the wilderness because they refuse to die to themselves. Our spirits have been set free, but our souls can remain in slavery. Freed from their shackles and fed the food of angels, the Hebrew slaves were longing to go back for the onions and leeks of Egypt at the first test. Jesus was in the wilderness for testing. He was fully aware that He was entitled to all of the authority in the universe. The devil offered Him the kingdoms of the world, but the Son declined in favor of pleasing His Father. He proved Himself through what He suffered.

It's easy to fall into that syndrome of, "I'm dying here, God; I need a word. God, I need a prophecy. God, I need some manna. God, come to do a miracle." That's a slave's way of thinking. Who is the servant of the Lord with the word of the Lord in His mouth? That person is a son. That person is you. Jesus came out of His test in the power of the Spirit. First after His baptism in the Jordan, and then after His burial in the grave, the Father delegated the authority of Heaven to His proven vessel.

BRINGING MANY SONS TO GLORY

When Jesus cried out, *"It is finished,"* He opened the way for us to enter the realm of His glory. This glory began at the cross, but it did not end there. As we respond to His invitation, we are becoming sons of glory, commended to God and filled with His strength, the same power by which the Spirit raised the Son up from the grave. We have been crucified and buried with Him—and raised up with Him into heavenly places:

> *It wasn't so long ago that you were mired in that old stagnant life of sin. You let the world, which doesn't know the first thing about living, tell you how to live. You filled your lungs with polluted unbelief, and then exhaled disobedience. We all did it, all of us doing what we felt like doing, when we felt like doing it, all of us in the same boat. It's a wonder God didn't lose His temper and do away with the whole lot of us. Instead, immense in mercy and with an incredible love, He embraced us. He took our sin-dead lives and made us alive in Christ. He did all this on His own, with no help from us! Then He picked us up and set us down in highest heaven in company with Jesus, our Messiah* (Ephesians 2:1-6 TM).

We are drawn to the cross to die with Him there. It is only through His death that we are raised up and gain access to grace in which we can stand:

> *Therefore, having been justified by faith, we have peace with God through our Lord Jesus Christ, through whom also we have access by faith into this grace in which we stand, and rejoice in hope of the glory of God* (Romans 5:1-2).

While we still have life in our mortal flesh, we are abiding in the finished work of Calvary. This is what Jesus meant when He said, *"If anyone desires to come after Me, let him deny himself, and take up his cross, and follow Me"* (Matt. 16:24).

Christ *"is the radiance of the glory of God and the exact imprint of His nature, and He upholds the universe by the word of his power. After making purification for sins, He sat down at the right hand of the Majesty on high"* (Heb. 1:3 ESV). He is greater in glory than Moses just as the second Testament is more glorious than the first, because the blood of bulls and goats could not redeem man from sin or wash guilty a conscience and bring about new birth (see Heb. 3:3). Jesus received glory because He suffered (see Heb. 2:19). He was received into glory when He ascended from the Mount in Jerusalem (see 1 Tim. 3:16). He is bringing many sons to glory (see Heb. 2:10). All of creation yearns to see them.

THE WAY UP IS DOWN

Jesus' mission meant leaving the glories of Heaven and coming down to us—as one of us. Imagine that! The King of glory as an ordinary man. He made Himself lower than the angels He created. He donned a servant's sandals and walked in our midst.

[A]lthough He existed in the form of God, did not regard equality with God a thing to be grasped, but emptied Himself, taking the form of a bond-servant, and being made in the likeness of men. Being found in appearance as a man, He humbled Himself by becoming obedient to the point of death, even death on a cross. For this reason also, God highly exalted Him, and bestowed on Him the name which is above every name (Philippians 2:6-9 NASB).

In God's Kingdom business, the way up is down. The way to glory is...down to the dust. I (Mahesh) remember when I first got filled with the Holy Ghost. I was so fired up. God spoke to me and said, "I am sending you on a mission. You are going to be my ambassador of love." I liked the sound of that. Before I knew it, I was led to a position in a state institution for the profoundly disabled. I was with "children" who were thirty years old according to the calendar, but less than two years old mentally. Many did not have any control over their toilet functions, so part of my job was cleaning up after them.

Have you ever cleaned up after a group of thirty-year-olds who consider themselves babies? They thought nothing of taking their excrement and smearing it on me; to them, it was playtime.

"Lord, you know how sensitive I am to bad smells."

"Love them. I am a Father to the fatherless. I'm going to anoint you. You just love them."

As I served there, I came to see that these people were truly orphaned in the sense that their parents did not want anything to do with them. They had been signed over to the custody of the state. Some of these children would never see their parents again. But the Lord had said, "Love them." That is what I did. And even the smell ceased to affect me.

The Holy Spirit is allergic to pride and competition, envy and jealousy, self-sufficiency and self-promotion. He wants to dwell in earthen vessels, but He cannot dwell in a vessel that is full of self. So to prepare us for His indwelling, He sets us up for humbling in order to empty us and make room for His glory. Our job is to become servants. His job is to make us sons. Why did I expect Him to spare me from suffering when He was sending me as His ambassador to those suffering little ones? Like much of the Church, I was wanting to live in the second part of Philippians 3:20-21: *"For our citizenship is in heaven,"* where *"our lowly body...[will] be conformed to His glorious body."* But to get there, I was going to need to go through the same humble training as Jesus did. It was there I saw God do amazing miracles. That was the very place He began to anoint me for ministry with power.

IN THE CROSS

Our Christian faith, a so-called "religion," is not a religion at all. It is a relationship of supernatural dimension. This salvation Christ supplies makes even suffering a floodplain where we can move from pool to pool, drinking out of heaven's oceans. Crucifying our own flesh does not imply simply disciplining ourselves to refrain from sin. It means that we have allowed the life of Another to be substituted for our own. This substitution is what completes or fills up the sufferings of the Son of God. He lives in us instead, residing where we once did.

The Spirit who raised Christ from the dead is transforming sons to match His likeness, clothed in His image, and empowered to manifest His Kingdom to the world around us in signs and wonders. Miracles are not the proof of our abiding as much as they are *"signs following"* (Mark 16:20 KJV), a demonstration and witness of the fact that His Kingdom has begun to invade! This keeps us *in* the cross, not merely within sight of it. Nothing in creation, not even the angels, show the excellence of majesty that Calvary does. There is no perfection of love, revealing of mystery or triumph of power greater than the Cross on which Jesus died. The cross has become the benchmark of creation.

Old-time surveyors chiseled benchmarks into something fixed so that a leveling rod could be repositioned in exactly the same place every time. With the cross as our benchmark, we see clearly what is crooked and what is straight. The cross is the end of all that has gone wrong and the beginning of all that has been made right. Fanny Crosby, the hymn-writer of the 19th century, put it all into a song:

Jesus, keep me near the cross,
There a precious fountain—
Free to all, a healing stream—
Flows from Calvary's mountain.
In the cross, in the cross,
Be my glory ever;
Till my raptured soul shall find
Rest beyond the river.
Near the cross! O Lamb of God,
Bring its scenes before me;
Help me walk from day to day,
With its shadows o'er me.[3]

ENDNOTES

1. From *The Dream of the Rood,* lines 78-86. Translation copyright © 1982, Jonathan A. Glenn. Used by permission.

2. St. Augustine identified the Spirit as the bond of love in his treatise, *On the Trinity,* discussed as follows in Alister E. McGrath, *Christian Theology: An Introduction,* 4th ed.

(Malden, MA: Wiley-Blackwell Publishing, Ltd., 2007), 239. "The Spirit is what is common to the Father and Son. The Father is only the Father of the Son, and the Son only the Son of the Father; the Spirit, however, is the Spirit of both Father and Son, binding them together in a bond of love."

3. "Near the Cross," by Fanny J. Crosby and William H. Doane, 1869. Lyrics in the public domain.

CHAPTER 5

BLOOD AND GLORY

The young hero stripped himself—he, God Almighty—
strong and stout-minded. He mounted high gallows,
bold before many, when he would loose mankind.
I shook when that Man clasped me....
Rood was I reared. I lifted a mighty King....[1]

"You will conceive and have a son and call His
name Emmanuel—God with Us."[2]

That was the beginning. I suppose that even then I knew, though I was a virgin to this world in every aspect. Something within me testified. It was as if two voices were speaking, opposite though not opposing. One was the voice of my heart full of the wonder of the glory of God in the miracle He had wrought. The other a sense of awful dread of what that great news would ultimately mean to me, to my family, to my people, to the son of my womb. I remember the flashing eyes of the old priest Simeon when we brought our firstborn to be dedicated. There was no Emmanuel in Joseph's line, but the old priest was not surprised at all when he asked for the babe's name. Instead, he looked intently upon my newborn's peaceful round face and said the words that were their own fulfillment:

"This infant is destined to cause many in Israel to fall and rise. Also, He will be a sign that will be opposed."[3]

Then he looked at me and my heart split in two. It seemed the old priest hardly got the words out, they were so low. Yet they carried the force of a storm at sea.

"Indeed, a sword will pierce your own soul, too, so that the inner thoughts of many people might be revealed."

And I knew.

It wasn't the early days of His revealing. In fact, they seemed bright compared to what came at the last. On that day—the terrible one. I shudder now remembering and my breath still stops. It's a mother remembering the child of her body.

"My son! My firstborn. My own darling who was the apple of my mothering eye and the chief delight to my heart."

I would it had been me instead. They did crucify women, too, though it was rare. I suppose I hoped, somehow, still believed, there would be another way before it came. The last time I touched Him with my lips, those same that had pressed His soft brow as a babe, the same that had caressed His busy hands when He was a child, and brushed His cheek with its first sprig of beard; the last time when my son was still my son was on that terrible day. His blood was on my lips as John helped me away. I pressed blood-wet palms hard against my face, taking in the last smell of Him, the last living remnant of what had once been His life. As if somehow I might breathe Him back to me through that blood. As if I could have given Him birth again, as if I possessed the power of His life and could return it. I would not go from that place until He was gone. And still I screamed for them to let me take His body down and bring Him home with me. His last words were to me:

"Mother, behold your son."

John has become a son to me, and I live in his care though my eyes are now dim, and I am not long for this world. I could perceive all that took place on that terrible day only afterward, when He came to us. I know the truth, all of it now, and so I wait for our reunion. I know He is not mine as He once was. He is so much more, and that day is the center of the whole world, although the world is still His adversary.

The cries of "Crucify!" seemed impossible, and my world went black as the courtyard rang out with them. He had done nothing wrong. He was so far from my reach, standing with the crowd between us and the procurator there beside Him on the dais. He already dripped with blood. His hands that had rubbed my shoulders at the end of a day or brought me milk or took the hearth brush away and finished my chore for me—*"Sit down, Mother,"* He would tell me gently, *"Let Me do it for you"*—were bound in prisoner's ropes.

I had not seen Him since before the feast when He entered Jerusalem and was hailed with joyful shouting. I had wondered for a moment if, as the angel had said, His name would be great then. That perhaps He would in fact drive out the Romans and ascend the throne in triumph. My son, the king of Israel. I suppose we all entertained those thoughts, although He assured us, sometimes laughing at our serious projections, that it would never be. And we did think Him rash when He called our people "His kingdom" as if He were already king when He was only a rabbi. My son, the rabbi.

It wasn't until after that terrible day that even His own disbelieving brothers finally bowed the knee like Joseph and his sheaves, though we had seen His miracles. My son, the miracle worker—something every Jewish mother says. But mine was! We stood huddled together on the wind-whipped hill. I had died a thousand times already since the morning sacrifice. He was not recognizable anymore by then. His face and hair were like those of a beast for slaughter. And yet He lived on as they hung Him up before us.

I know what unutterable means. Trembling with involuntary seizing from His loss of blood, His eyes swollen nearly shut from their beatings. Roman boots and the soles of priests' sandals were red where they had followed us on the road. I wondered if they noticed at all when they took their shoes off that night. He would not have suffered so long if He were not so strong. He was a carpenter's son. He was undeterred even after shock took Him over. I suppose He had thought about it so long that once it began He was resigned.

But I was not resigned.

I kept hoping my eyes lied through their blur of tears. That it was a horrible trance brought on by my worst fears and doubt. I beheld Him and I remember wondering how He would ever recover from the scars His torturers had made on Him. Would He ever again have the same face His mother knew so well? He set it like flint and they sharpened their swords on Him. I would have had Him back even at the very last had it been possible. Even if He had never fully recovered and I would have to nurse him, an invalid, at least He would have been at home with me. John assured me that on the night He was betrayed He told them exactly what would take place, though they, like me, didn't grasp it until we witnessed it with our eyes. John told me they fell asleep in spite of themselves. I slept little in those days. The air was tense with assurance that we were coming to some kind of climax. But no one could have convinced me it would be that. If I had known, I would have poisoned Judas' soup one of those times I let him into our house. He never fooled me, and I told my son as much. In those days I simply thought He was not listening to the warnings of his mother.

"Eloi! Eloi! Lama sabachthani?"[4]

He was no longer connected to earth, and I was no longer His mother. His outstretched limbs, blackened with bruising, skin hanging in shreds like the corners of a too-much-used prayer shawl, ragged, holy, and dyed red with self giving, were bringing the cosmos back to its Creator. My son was bringing many sons home to His Father. The brief race we ran together as mother and son, watching Him grow up like a green tree, was run. The victor's wreath they gave Him was a crown of thorns, and He wore it that day like a young hero. The cheering crowd that should have hailed Him to His race's end only shouted abuses. Still He ran on toward the finish. My Son, the Hero.

But He was not mine—He belonged instead to Him. He belongs to us.

The glory of God is to share His glory with man. The divine exchange for man was settled before the foundation of the world. In that pre-time of perfection, the Father had you already formed in His mind. You existed to Him before there ever was a single cell of your mortal substance. He ordained to have eternal fellowship with you. With the future advent of sin set to bring separation in God-man communion, the remedy was the blood of Jesus. He made the plan to draw you into His life-giving embrace. This is the glory of our salvation.

This divine mystery of the inexplicable greatness of God is majestic and intimate. The Son predetermined to take on human flesh and blood to secure your future glory. The destiny of man—the total of his being, is glory. It is the glory of a son in his father. It is the glory of Christ in His Incarnation as a Man, and His return to the glory He had before, in the beginning. Jesus' mission was planned in the Godhead before anything was created: before angels, before heavens and earth, before man, before there was any good or evil. Before sin. Before alienation.

The story unfolds in the shades of Eden. It begins with a revelation: that the life of the soul is in the blood. God makes the first move as He shows the power of life in the blood. Before their separation, man and woman were majestic, innocent, perfect, and clothed in glory. God sacrificed an innocent life to make coverings for Adam and Eve after their shame was exposed and they were found naked. As the life in the blood of an innocent life provides a covering for them, the greatest love story ever told is in its first chapter.

The Lord told Cain, *"The voice of your brother's blood cries out to Me from the ground"* (Gen. 4:10). Blood has a voice. Life is in the blood (see Lev. 17:11). Noah offered blood sacrifice for the saving of his family in the flood. A ram was provided for Abraham as an exchange for the life of Isaac, the son of promise. Since the beginning of time and human history there is a radical link between the blood exchange for the life of the soul and the abiding Presence of God called His glory. The blood makes the way. Blood atonement was the center of Tabernacle worship whereupon the cloud of God's Presence abode in the tent of meeting. He moved into a more permanent house with the completion and dedication of Solomon's Temple. The *chavod,* weighty Presence, came down in such power that the priests fell down in that glory:

> *When Solomon had ended his prayer, fire came down*
> *from heaven and consumed the burnt offering and the*
> *sacrifices, and the glory of the Lord filled the temple.*
> *And the priests could not enter the house of the Lord,*

because the glory of the Lord filled the Lord's house
(2 Chronicles 7:1-2 ESV).

The epic continues down through God's relationship with people of faith until at last He appears in the flesh and begins the march to Calvary. The next chapter of the glory story climaxes when Jesus, our High Priest, cries: *"It is finished!"* indicating atonement is accomplished forever, for all. Christ's intercession through His blood sends the Holy Spirit to seek us out. He knocks on the door of our hearts and reveals Christ in order to bring us home. It's usually a surprise visit, or at least it appears that way to us. Sometimes it is in the middle of painful or even frightening circumstances that He takes opportunity. He comes looking for us.

But that is not the end of the story. The Prince of Heaven ascends to the Father. Offering the blood of His sacrifice to purge the court of Heaven once desecrated in the rebellion of lucifer, Jesus takes up His priestly ministry of intercession for all who run for refuge to His blood. At that point the Spirit is poured out from the fount of holy grace and descends on the Church in its natal hour in Jerusalem. In tongues of fire and ecstatic Presence, the newborn Bride of the Begotten One is wrapped in heavenly garments as she is clothed with the Spirit. It is her nuptial *mikva*.

The Spirit's garment of glory is not only external, as it was under the first covenant, now He has entered into her heart. It is the demonstration that she has become the light of the world to be on display. Through her, the world will receive knowledge of the soon coming King. The Spirit is the warranty of the Father's promise. He is the sign of the Bridegroom's pledge: "In My Father's house are many mansions, I go to prepare a place for you and I will return to take you to be with Me where I am!" (see John 14).

The epicenter of glory is the blood of the Lamb where life for humanity's soul is secured. Here is love's final destination. It's a song to be sung by men and angels forever. The song of the Bride and her Bridegroom. The song of the Lamb.

THE BLOOD SPEAKS

During a Watchman Tour to Israel we were privileged to get to know Morrie and his family. Morrie is Iranian and was raised in the Muslim faith. In 2001 Morrie's business came under investigation and the pressure pushed him to the brink of collapse. With the possibility of prison looming, he cried out, "God, if You are there either take me or make me." A supernatural peace so deep and so real wrapped around him like a covering. It settled down and stayed on him for three days.

That was the beginning for Morrie. He received Christ, and the series of events that followed includes miracle after miracle of deliverance and testimony in the midst of challenges and setbacks equally astounding. Today he is spreading the Gospel to his native people. Upon hearing his story, we realized that the atmosphere of supernatural peace that steered him through the trials and trouble was the effective presence of the blood of Jesus working on his behalf prior to Morrie's knowledge of it! That peace was settled at Calvary where God was pleased *"through Him to reconcile to Himself all things, whether on earth or in heaven, making peace by the blood of His cross"* (Col. 1:20 ESV).

At the set time, God favored Morrie, and the blood broke through the darkness, speaking from the throne of Heaven on his behalf. The Spirit descended, revealing Christ, and brought Morrie into adoption. The blood is God's line in the sands of the desert of sin. God gave the Hebrews understanding that innocent blood possessed power to draw God's Presence near in judgment. God exerted great Personal energy to deliver Israel from slavery in Egypt. That energy expelled His people out of bondage. The Passover blood was placed on every home. Whole families, whole tribes, were covered. That divine sanction reestablished fellowship between earth and heaven, between God and His man. Innocent blood must be responded to by the Holy One—the blood makes way for the Spirit of holiness.

As Egypt came under judgment, the Passover blood made the distinction. There was a radical difference between two communities: One placed the blood on display; the other held up idols. It meant life for one and death for the other. The nation of Israel was baptized in the sea and wrapped in the cloud of God's glory as He led them out of bondage and into their promised inheritance. What He did for Israel in Egypt, He has done for all in Christ. That is the glory of Calvary.

ESCAPE FROM DEATH

In the consecration of the Levitical priests for the work of service, the blood atonement was brought before the presence of the Lord. The priests laid their hands on the head of the sacrifice and imputed the power of their sins and the sins of the people upon it:

> *Aaron and his sons shall put their hands on the head of the bull. Then you shall kill the bull before the Lord, by the door of the tabernacle of meeting. You shall take some of the blood of the bull and put it on the horns of the altar with your finger, and pour all the blood beside the base of the altar* (Exodus 29:10-12).

The Hebrew words for justice and bloodshed sound the same.[5] The language God gave the Hebrews speaks in such a way that whenever bloodshed is mentioned, justice whispers, too. Or whenever justice is called for, the necessity of blood echoes in the words. The blood says, "Justice is satisfied." *"There is therefore now no condemnation to those who are in Christ Jesus"* (Rom. 8:1 ESV).

The first time "glory" is mentioned in the Bible, Jacob is speaking about the fate of his sons: *"Let not my soul enter their council; let not my glory be united to their assembly; for in their anger they slew a man"* (Gen. 49:6). Jacob's "glory" is the honor of his name among present and future generations. God's glory is the same. He reveals His glory to reveal His Name and demonstrate His character. He is jealous for His reputation in the sense that He is completely holy and He will not give His honor (glory) to that which is unholy or unrighteous. Glory, blood, and communion between persons are intermingled. There is only one blood that brings fellowship with glory: Jesus' innocent blood. It is the unbreakable bond creating ongoing communion.

The sin that entered the human race through Adam had to be effectively and permanently dealt with in full—spiritually, legally, redemptively, and relationally—in order to restore our destiny. The perfect plan was devised and settled in Heaven before the foundation of the world. When the Father had you in mind, the Son volunteered for the mission necessary to achieve it and the Spirit said, "I'll go with you." O, the blood! O, the glory! The Lamb would be slain for the sin of the whole world. What love! What sacrifice! What majesty! What power!

THERE'S POWER IN THE BLOOD

When Christ became sin, there was an exchange, an infusion, and the result is life abundant and eternal. We can think of enzymatic action as a parable. Enzymes can be used to clean up a chemical spill or remove the stains from your favorite shirt. When enzymes are applied, they subsume the particles to such an extent that the offending elements cease to exist. There is a final by-product of the action—oxygen, the breath of life. We might liken this picture to our justification that comes to us in Christ. So effective is the redemptive work of the King of Glory that rudimental things reflect the glory of the Lamb and of His Spirit!

As the blood fulfilled its mission we received the breath of life—the Holy Spirit. It happened completely when you received Jesus as Savior. The working power of the blood is a present reality ongoing day to day. The Book of Romans speaks of walking in the Spirit and putting to death the works of the flesh. The old man, our corrupt nature into which every person is born, has died—executed for sin in Christ on the cross. In his place a new creation in the express image of God is being formed through the ministry of the Holy Spirit. As you are led by Him, you are allowing His transforming ministry to continue in you. God forbid that any of us who are partakers of this great mystery should give life to the old nature by walking after the flesh.

The High Priest of our confession is ministering before the Father on our behalf day by day. The Father has sent the Spirit into our hearts to fulfill the ministry of Christ toward us. The Spirit who searches the heart and mind of God is in fact God Himself resident in you. He knows you intimately. He intercedes in each of us according to God's will. The Spirit builds the Body of Christ. He prepares the Bride for the Son. We are being transformed from glory to glory into the same image.

COVERED IN BLOOD

Aaron and his sons shall put their hands on the head of the ram. Then you shall kill the ram, and take some of its blood and put it on the tip of the right ear of Aaron and on the tip of the right ear of his sons, on the thumb of their right hand and on the big toe of their right foot, and sprinkle the blood all around on the altar. And you shall take some of the blood that is on the altar, and some of the anointing oil, and sprinkle it on Aaron and on his garments, on his sons and on the garments of his sons with him; and he and his garments shall be hallowed, and his sons and his sons' garments with him (Exodus 29:19-21).

Those first priestly garments were but shadows of the spiritual coverings given to the saints. We are covered from head to toe! First by the blood and then with the Spirit. The blood enables your spiritual ears to hear God's voice. Your hands become the hands of Christ extended in divine authority and power. Your feet have been sanctified, prepared with the Gospel that speaks peace through His blood. Jesus is our High Priest and we are His "sons" in the manner of the priesthood of Aaron. The cross makes provision for the Spirit to be poured out, clothing all who would receive His sacrifice. This clothing from on high prefigures what shall be in the resurrection:

For we know that if the tent that is our earthly home is destroyed, we have a building from God, a house not made with hands, eternal in the heavens. For in this tent we groan, longing to put on our heavenly dwell-

ing, if indeed by putting it on we may not be found naked (2 Corinthians 5:1-3).

Some of the blood was dabbed on the earlobe and thumb and toe of each priest just as it was placed on the doors of every house during Passover. The blood changes everything and presents us perfect to God. The Spirit rests on the blood and we enter communion with Him. The blood of Jesus is fresh today. When we feel His Presence, when we see His miracles, it is because the complete work of Calvary has affected a cosmic change that makes the glory toward us possible. Jesus said, "You shall receive power." Power to become the evidence, the witness, the testimony of His redemptive work manifest in the earth. The power to become the sons of God.

Get a fresh awareness of the power and precious presence of the blood that speaks for you, hour by hour, in every situation (see Heb. 12:24). We have been covered by the blood and immersed in the cloud. Not painted over, but purged, recreated in the death and burial of Christ. Not just surrounded by the cloud of His Spirit, infused with Him, more powerful and intimate, more visible and imminent than when the glory cloud and the pillar of fire rested on the camp of Israel!

CLOTHED IN GLORY

For Aaron's sons you shall make tunics, and you shall make sashes for them. And you shall make hats for them, for glory and beauty. So you shall put them on Aaron your brother and on his sons with him. You shall anoint them, consecrate them, and sanctify them, that they may minister to Me as priests (Exodus 28:40-41).

I (Bonnie) was returning from a visit to the Kotel, the wall of prayer, in Jerusalem. My eyes fell on the *tzittzit*—the linen threads that hang from the corners of the Jewish prayer shawl—of a young man in front of me. The threads were exquisite. One thread of deep indigo mixed among white ones of extraordinary length literally danced on the wind as the man went up the road. The threads seemed to be telling a story. I thought of the woman in the Gospels who had a lingering, debilitating infirmity. I could see her in the crowd pressed around Jesus two thousand years before. She reached out, her fingertips just able to catch one of those threads on the *tallit* Jesus wore. Her fingers holding fast to the end of a single thread extending from the edge of His garment, Jesus felt divine virtue drawn out by someone whose life literally hung by that thread. Her faith connected to a thread of His glory and it was enough to heal her completely. It would have been against Jewish custom for the woman to have grabbed Jesus' body. But she could touch His robe:

> *A woman who had had a hemorrhage for twelve years, and could not be healed by anyone, came up behind Him and touched the border of His garment; instantly her hemorrhaging stopped. Jesus asked, "Who touched Me?" When they all denied doing it, Peter said, "Rabbi! The crowds are hemming you in and jostling you!" But Jesus said, "Someone did touch Me, because I felt power go out of me." Seeing she could not escape notice, the woman, quaking with fear, threw herself down before Him and confessed in front of everyone why she had touched Him and how she had been instantly healed. He said to her, "My daughter, your trust has saved you; go in peace"* (Luke 8:43-48 ESV).

Mystical sages in Judaism write: *"He who keeps the command-ments grabs the Divine presence. This is the meaning of tzittzit."*[6] Jesus speaks of wearing the tallit with the tzittzit: *"Everything they do is done for men to see: They make their phylacteries wide and the tassels on their garments long"* (Matt. 23:5). We may assume that Jesus wore a tallit in keeping with the commandment: *"You shall make tassels on the four corners of the clothing with which you cover yourself"* (Deut. 22:12). In this verse the word for tassels is from a root equivalent to glory or making great in stature or honor.[7] Mark 6:56 records that: *"They begged Him to let them touch even the tzittzit on His robe, and all who touched it were healed."*[8]

The sages understood the tzittzit as symbolic of God's glory, divine threads of life connected to the Presence of the Lord. The Hebrew words for covering, edge of a garment, wings and glory are from the same root.[9] The hem of a garment is the place the tzittzit extends from.

According to Daniel 7:9 and Psalm 104:2 God wraps Himself in light. It describes the glory surrounding the Lord. To put on the tallit was to put on the word of the Lord, His commandments, His righteousness, His power and authority—His *chashmal*, the heav-enly illumination as lightening coming from the throne.[10] Bound by his prayer and the tallit, the four knotted tassels were a reminder and a witness to the wearer. But it wasn't the garment, it was the glory of the One wearing it whose power to heal emanated from those edges of His robe.

The Lord of Glory comes down on Sinai with a trumpet fanfare and rumbling thunder and a light show that shakes the wilderness and makes the great rocks crumble. When God called Moses up into the shekinah on Sinai He brought Moses under the cover of His robe of light and life. While mountains are trembling all around him, Moses cries, "Show me Your glory!" God hides him in the cleft of a rock and covers him with His hand. "You cannot see My face and live," God replies. God is pointing to the Day when men would see His glory in the face of the Nazarene. The glory saturated Moses' entire being and shown out of him when he came down to the people.

The Glory of Sinai came down to the Tent of Meeting. He gave gem-bedecked robes to His ministers and sprinkled them with the blood of atonement from the hattat-offering (decontamination-offering).[11] Then He poured the scented oil of anointing on them and filled the Tent with His cloud (see Lev. 9:22-23).

HEAVENLY GLORY

The physical garments the Israelites wore were reminders of their relationship with Heaven. The tzittzit and a blue cord on the hem of the garment of prayer was commanded by the Lord:

> *Speak to the children of Israel: Tell them to make tassels* [tzittzit] *on the corners* [wings] *of their garments* [coverings] *throughout their generations, and to put a blue thread in the tassels of the corners. And you shall have the tassel, that you may look upon it and remember all the commandments of the Lord and do them..."* (Numbers 15:38-39).

The blue thread is the *shamash*, the servant, and it is the royal color of the King. The Servant strand is wrapped around the other strands equivalent to the numerical values of the first and last letters in the name of the Lord, *Adonai Echad*, the Lord is One. The numerical value of the words for *tzittzit* and *echad* is 613, the same as the number of the commandments in the Law of Moses. When the wearer looks upon the tassels he awakens his heart to the love of the commandments and obedience toward them (see John 14:15).

The blue thread was "given to look on" just as Christ was given to be seen among men as the only Begotten of the Father. Jesus became flesh and dwelt among men so that we might see His glory. Jesus is the blue cord, the Darling of Heaven, woven into the fabric of humanity that we might be joined to the Lord and share in His glory. Zechariah prophesied a day that the tallit wearers would be sought by the nations for the Presence of God they carried:

> *Thus saith the Lord of hosts; In those days it shall come to pass, that ten men shall take hold out of all languages of the nations, even shall take hold of the corner of the garment of him that is a Jew, saying, "We will go with you: for we have heard that God is with you"* (Zechariah 8:23 KJV).

The final image of Christ coming in glory is the image of Him on clouds of power wearing a blood-dipped garment:

> *"Then I saw heaven opened, and there before me was a white horse. Sitting on it was the One called Faithful and True, and it is in righteousness that He passes judgment and goes to battle. His eyes were like a fiery flame, and on his head were many royal crowns. And He had a name written which no one knew but Himself. He was wearing a robe that had been soaked in blood, and the name by which He is called is, 'The Word of God'"* (Revelation 19:11-13 NIV).

His covering, symbolic of the Holy Spirit and the glory, is dipped in His blood. The Greek word used here for robe is the same word used to refer to a tallit. The blood and the glory, Christ and the Spirit, are One, present and working in great power and redemption to bring forth the will of the Father in glory on earth.

OVER ALL THE GLORY

The Tabernacle represents mortal human life in this temporary world. The ark in the Tabernacle contained manna, Aaron's rod that budded, and the tablets. In Solomon's Temple, the pattern of the glory of Heaven to come, only the tablets were left in the ark. They symbolize Christ in us in the resurrection and our being fully clothed at last with the same glory. Ephesians speaks of this clothing now as our armor against spiritual forces of wickedness (see Eph. 6:11).

The layers of covering over the Tabernacle, from innermost to external, picturize man in communion with God. The four layers are woven linen, goats' hair, ram's wool dyed red, and oiled badger skins. The innermost covering is woven linen. It is a type of the righteous character of the Son and the righteous acts of the saints: *"This is the covenant I will make with them after that time, says the Lord. I will put my laws in their hearts, and I will write them on their minds"* (Heb. 10:16).

A supernatural transformation occurs when one receives Christ into his or her heart. The curtains around the ark were woven with cherubim in rich colors of red, blue, and purple on pure white. They represent the glory of God in the redeemed soul as the dwelling place of God. The covering is the glory of God and the glory of a pure heart woven together in communion. Ezekiel speaks of the Tabernacle glory: *"I clothed you also with embroidered cloth and shod you with badger's skin. I wrapped you in fine linen and covered you with silk"* (Ezek. 16:10).

Over the linen is a covering of goats' hair. The black hair of goats calls to mind the Shulamite in the Song of Solomon: *"I am dark but lovely, O daughters of Jerusalem, like the tents of Kedar, like the curtains of Solomon"* (Song of Sol. 1:5).

The tents of Kedar belonged to the Gentiles. Some of the earliest seekers of Christ were the Gentile kings who followed His star to Bethlehem. The Shulamite contrasts her soul, dark like the Kenite tents, typifying man's old nature, with the royal tent, the nature of Christ, in which the king was awaiting his bride according to Eastern custom. Our "goat" nature was dealt with when Christ became the scapegoat and released us from our sins.

The Shulamite is made "comely" through the comeliness bestowed upon her as a garment in preparation for her wedding.

> *I will greatly rejoice in the LORD; my soul shall exult in my God, for He has clothed me with the garments of salvation; He has covered me with the robe of righteousness, as a bridegroom decks himself like a priest with a beautiful headdress, and as a bride adorns herself with her jewels* (Isaiah 61:10 ESV).

It is the comeliness of Christ's nature imputed to those who exercise faith in Him through His blood that prepares us for union with Him.

The blood makes way for the Presence of God to descend and transform us from the inside out. Over the layer of goat's hair are rams' skins dyed red. They are the type of the blood covering. That provision makes the interweaving of glory possible. The constant testimony of the blood in the heart of the believer secures the ongoing Presence of God's Spirit. The intermingling of the blood and glory belongs to both the Bride and the Bridegroom: *"These are the ones who have come out of the great tribulation and have washed their robes and made them white in the blood of the Lamb"* (Rev. 7:14 ESV), and *"He was wearing a robe that had been soaked in blood, and the name by which He is called is; 'The Word of God'"* (Rev. 19:13).

The top layer that covered the Tabernacle was made of oiled badger skins. Weatherproofed with oil to fend against the damaging elements of nature, those skins protected the inner coverings of beauty and glory. The oil is a type of the anointing continually replenished on all who are being led by the Spirit of God. The anointing of the Holy Spirit every hour makes real power available to you. You can think the thoughts of God. You can understand how to approach your daily situation with His heavenly perspective. You can have supernatural wisdom. You can hear His voice and walk in the power of the Spirit to accomplish what is set before you. You can live a naturally supernatural, supernaturally natural life every day: *"Not by might, nor by power, but by My Spirit,' says the Lord"* (Zech. 4:6).

ENTER HIS REST

The Great Lover of our souls watches daily at the gates of His city. He is looking for us to come and sit in His shade. He is longing to feed us with His hand. He carried the weight of the world on the cross and His Presence is ready to lift you up in His strength. He went to the cross looking forward to the joy that His victory there would obtain. That love, that care, that rest, that provision, that strength, and that joy are His gifts to each of us. You are all His desire. Let Him be yours.

Like the story of the woman with the issue of blood who took hold of the threads of glory that hung from the edge of His robe, though the crowd presses all around Him, when you reach out to touch His hem, He turns toward you and all His virtue runs to fill you up with His life. It's like a story with a happy end. With Jesus as your Lord, you are Ruth, the Moabite woman whose name is the word for friend.

It was harvest time. The famine in the House of Bread was over. Ruth's mother-in-law, Naomi, a widow like Ruth, was going home to Bethlehem. In spite of her own difficult circumstance, Ruth was going too. How could she leave Naomi to make the journey alone?

They arrived in Naomi's hometown with nothing but the clothes on their backs, with no one but each other to take care of them. But Ruth wasn't looking for a handout. So she went right to work in a neighborhood field picking up the leftover grain. It happened that the Lord was arranging everything behind the scenes. When lunchtime came, the field's owner, a prominent man named Boaz, noticed Ruth and asked her over for lunch. Ruth's good reputation was already news and Boaz gave special instructions that his crew leave lots of grain for Ruth to retrieve.

Barley harvest came and went and so did wheat harvest. At the end of the season, there was always a big celebration. Naomi said, "Listen, get dressed up and go down to the shindig with the others." In fact Naomi advised Ruth to let Boaz know that Ruth was available! So Ruth did as she was advised. Around midnight after lots of eating and drinking, Boaz lay down for a snooze. And Ruth laid down where he was. It was a pretty bold thing to do in those days. It just might have ruined Ruth's reputation. But she was trusting in God. As dawn approached, Boaz awoke and turned over to find Ruth beside him! He didn't send her home empty handed. He also gave her a pledge.

The story ends with a fairytale wedding. An estate, an inheritance, a family and children and just about everything good you can imagine. But even that's not the end of it all. As it turns out, God had been watching Ruth. Before she ever fell on bad times, the Lord had a different end in mind. Her new husband was a patriarch in a very special family. About a year after they married, Ruth gave birth to a son. That boy would grow up to be the grandfather of David, the king of Israel. Who would ever imagine that Ruth's destiny was planned so well?

Her story is yours. Jesus is your Boaz. Naomi is a type of the Holy Spirit who leads us to our spiritual inheritance. No matter if you are a man or a woman, this is a story about your redemption. It's the story of good that God has in mind for your life. It's harvest time in the earth. His workers are entering the fields and He's waiting for you to join them. He's had His eye on you for good all along. Remember the advice from Naomi: "Lay down at His feet and wait until morning. He will tell you what to do." He won't send you away empty. He has better plans than you know. Stretch out your hands and He'll fill them with plenty of good things from His storehouse.

Remember what Ruth said to Boaz? "Spread the wings of your robe over me" (see Ruth 3:9). This is your story. You have been purchased and given a full inheritance. The Spirit has come to take away your barrenness. He has spread out His wings like a wedding canopy and invites you to sit down in His shade. You can rest in the cloud of His glory until He does for you all He has promised.

ENDNOTES

1. From *The Dream of the Rood,* lines 39-42, 44. Translation copyright © 1982, Jonathan A. Glenn. Used by permission.

2. See Matthew 1:23.

3. See Luke 2:34-35.

4. Mark 15:34.

5. See Isaiah 5:7. Justice is the Hebrew word *mishpat* and Bloodshed is the Hebrew *mispach*.

6. Zohar (Splendor or Radiance) 1:23b.

7. See Gadal http://www.studylight.org/isb/view.cgi?number =001431.

8. David H. Stern, trans. *Jewish New Testament* (Jerusalem: Jewish New Testament Publications, 1989).

9. See Kanaph http://www.studylight.org/isb/view.cgi?number =03671.

10. See Chashmal http://www.studylight.org/isb/view.cgi?number =02830.

11. *Hattat* was formerly translated as "sin-offering" but is now understood to be a purification offering that decontaminates the sanctuary and individuals. "Central to the *hattat*-offering is the use of its blood as a detergent to absorb and purify the pollution that has accrued in the sanctuary." See commentary on Leviticus 4:3 in *The Five Books of Moses: Genesis, Exodus, Numbers, Deuteronomy*, trans. Everett Fox (New York: Schocken, 1995), 518.

CHAPTER 6

GLORY IN BATTLE

But there eager ones came from afar
to that noble one....
They took there Almighty God,
lifted him from that grim torment....
They laid there the limb-weary one, stood at his body's head;
beheld they there heaven's Lord, and he himself rested there,
worn from that great strife.
Then they worked him an earth-house,
men in the slayer's sight carved it from bright stone,
set in it the Wielder of Victories.
Then they sang him a sorrow-song,
sad in the eventide, when they would go again
with grief from that great Lord. He rested
there, with small company.[1]

† † † † † † † † † † † † †

We ended Uncle Silas' *shiva* today. For the second time. We don't mourn now as we once did. We know

now he's not dead—just sleeping for a bit after a long full life. I'm sure it's no coincidence that Uncle fell asleep right before the New Year this time. The customary mourning period was one day, not seven. Just long enough for us to eat "the meal of comfort" brought by neighbors. Some soft tears glistened. He had told us he couldn't wait anymore. So we drank to his health and about "died" ourselves from laughter, rejoicing for him. Before, that would have offended.

I remember our mood the first time we buried him. It was the difference of life and death. He was young then and not yet wed. We marvel how different Silas was his second time around! We are all very different because of him, different about everything. We know now. We have seen with our eyes, we have held in our hands, the reality of the world *Mashiach* rules over. This temporary one is but a sigh in the night by comparison to the One coming.

Uncle Silas showed up zigzagging down between the houses just after the earthquake. I laugh out loud thinking of it. People were gasping and darting away in terror. There he was, walking up our road, wrestling to get out of his grave clothes. No one dared to help. Touch a dead man walking? Who had ever seen such a thing? The city was already in an uproar over the Nazarene's crucifixion. His disciples had gone into hiding.

As soon as he got his face free, Silas burst out laughing. The same uproarious laughter that used to echo down these alleys where he was born, lived, and had died too soon. A God-fearer, he was meticulous in keeping the commandments. Uncle Silas went to Temple and *mikva,* paid his tithe, and gave to the poor. He was quick to lend his strong shoulder whenever there was heavy lifting to be done. All that did little to soften his temper when it occasionally got away from him. His debtors knew to steer clear during the feasts. Too much wine didn't mix well with old injustices. But when he did go too far, Uncle was so remorseful. He'd make up for it by doing some difficult task for the affronted neighbor. I loved him.

My own father, his brother, could do little to console my agony back then. The wall of a neighbor's house had fallen on him while repairing a place that sagged beneath a roof beam. Silas' bruised, unresponsive body grew more pale and thin by the day. Everybody was praying. I clung to his limp hand, hoping God would awaken him if I refused to eat. It was just impossible that my uncle—who lifted a neighbor's ox out of a miry pit during the latter-rain flooding—could lie there so unfinished, so helpless as if asleep. He had been invincible. Father refused to let me carry on like that after a day or two.

I recognized Uncle immediately when he came staggering home. Cowering in our doorway, I wondered what had just happened. People were screaming as I looked up to see the mummy coming down the street. In an instant, I knew whose hands those were impatiently ripping off their bonds, hands that could bend bronze or hold mine so tenderly. Imagine a little girl of nine racing up the road to hug a living corpse. But I did with all my might. Unclean or not, my Uncle Silas was alive!

We made him tell it again and again. At supper, in the synagogue, while he finished a new wall or hoisted a beam over a doorframe, we children would find him and beg him to repeat the details.

"The righteous aren't dead," he'd say, his flashing grin crossing his face in confidence, his once-again bulging muscles at hard work. He'd look us in the eye, and silent thunder rumbled through our souls. My hair was standing on end in a mix of awe and joy. He was living proof of what he said.

"We were there, the lot of us," he'd turn again to his task, "many more than I could count. There was a great gulf, and we could hear cries of those on the other side." A shadow would cross his brow. He told me of a particular Sadducee whose cold heart and loud prayers made him hated by simple folk. The pompous fellow exacted ten times a fair interest of anyone making the mistake to accept his so-called charity when they got in a bind. "Don't think harshly of him now," Uncle Silas said. A tear of pity pushed out of his eye, and he didn't bother to hide it. "His exactors are even less merciful than he was." It seemed to leave him without words—that part of what he witnessed when we all thought Silas was just a decaying body in the family sepulcher.

"The powers that bound us in that place suddenly ceased to exist in His Presence. And we who had been weighted down by them were instantly loosed. Abraham, Moses, and all the rest kept telling us that He was coming. That He would bring us out in an exodus greater than that of our fathers from

Egypt!" Sometimes he would sadly trail off. "But the others," he would say, "those ones across the way..."

Never again did he turn angry when the feast wine flowed—and did it flow on the day of his wedding! Uncle Silas who was dead got a beautiful wife and had sons and daughters. Some of the neighbors still insist the whole thing was a trick. Silas said the sun shining in noonday strength is darkness compared to the light that flashed forth in Sheol that day. Death gasped when the Warrior broke in.

Even sadness for those left behind in darkness would vanish once Silas began describing *Mashiach*. "His hair flashed like lightening bolts. His eyes were flames hotter and brighter than hell itself— flames of burning love. His garment swirled about Him, swallowing up our grave." Uncle Silas would close his eyes and turn around in place. "Ten thousand New Year shofars and the shouts of Israel when Jericho fell are whispers in comparison!" Eyes wide again, he'd stop. "Suddenly here I was! Stumbling down our dusty street as if coming home from a day's work!"

The elders would ask Uncle Silas to stand up in the congregation and tell it all again. The congregation would whoop and cheer. There were Jews who hated us for sticking to what they insisted was the conspiracy of Peter and the others who had believed the Nazarene before He was executed for treason and blasphemy. He is the One we waited for.

"Don't be afraid of death or the men who peddle it," Uncle Silas told me. "The Righteous One has the last laugh! He finished it all! Took care of the whole thing for us! And all those mourners we used to hire? To sing over us when we died? Ha! What a waste of money!"

Biblical writers understood that the spiritual realm of angels and demons occupied a parallel reality and impacted the physical one where man dwells. Everything that we can see and touch is temporary, not eternal. *If you can see it, it will change.* However, *"the things which **are not seen** are eternal"* (2 Cor. 4:18). There are spiritual things that you cannot perceive with your natural senses but they are true realities. This is why it is vital to *develop your spiritual senses.*

There are two very real, eternal, spiritual kingdoms. One is all light, life, and love. One is reigned over in righteousness by the Prince of glory. The other is all darkness, wickedness, sin, and death. It is dominated by a perverse, tyrannical deceiver.

There is an enmity between these two rulers. It is a conflict that nothing will ever reconcile. One of these rulers is Sovereign God Almighty. His adversary is just a fallen angel. Satan means "opposer" or "adversary." This spiritual conflict affects the entire human race. Earth is the battleground, the human race is under siege by the enemy of God, and Christians are His spiritual warriors of light. We have come into harmony with the prayer Jesus taught His disciples to pray, acknowledging our Father in Heaven, praying His kingdom into the earth, and opposing forces of wickedness.

> *Our Father in heaven, hallowed be Your name. Your kingdom come. Your will be done on earth as it is in heaven. Give us this day our daily bread. And forgive us our debts, As we forgive our debtors. And do not*

*lead us into temptation, but deliver us from the evil
one. For Yours is the kingdom and the power and the
glory forever. Amen* (Matthew 6:9-14).

This is the ultimate prayer of spiritual warfare.

The Bible says that our wrestling match is not against persons
with bodies of flesh and blood, but against rulers with various realms
of authority, against the world dominators of the present darkness,
against spiritual forces of wickedness in the heavenlies (see Eph.
6:12). The battle pits us against satanic spiritual forces. The Holy
Spirit prepares and equips us for victory every time.

In ancient times people recognized this battle much more
readily. As one writer describes:

> The sky hung low over the ancient world. Traffic was
> heavy on the highway between heaven and earth.
> Gods and spirits thickly populated the upper air,
> where they stood in readiness to intervene at any mo-
> ment in the affairs of mortals. And demonic powers,
> emerging from the lower world or resident in remote
> corners of the earth were a constant menace to hu-
> man welfare. All nature was alive—alive with super-
> natural forces.[2]

God's victory plan is the cross and resurrection. That victory
subsumes everything else. There are four successive stages in Christ's
victory over satan. The conquest predicted in Genesis 3:15, "*He*
[Christ] *shall crush your* [satan's] *head*"; the conquest begun during
Jesus' earthly ministry as He cast out demons and healed the sick;
the conquest achieved as He suffered on the cross, "*that through
death He might destroy him who had the power of death, that is the
devil. And release those who through fear of death were all their lifetime*

subject to bondage" (Heb. 2:14-15); and the conquest confirmed and announced in His resurrection from the grave.

When Jesus mounted the cross, He despoiled the weaponry and authority of demonic rulers and presented them unmasked and conquered in complete humiliation before the cosmos. The cross provides satisfaction for all legal claims the adversary poses against us:

> [Christ] *has taken it out of the way, having nailed it to the cross. Having disarmed principalities and powers, He made a public spectacle of them, triumphing over them in it* (Colossians 2:14-15).

If people focus on wrestling with demons, they overlook the strategy needed in spiritual battle. The holy angels and the hierarchies of darkness all witnessed the undoing of satanic tyranny. The battle we face in this world is because satan has not yet conceded the defeat Christ has already dealt him.

Christ became the Firstborn from the grave, the Head of His body, the Church, and we all partake of Him. We are adopted as sons and become stewards of His creation. We are His ambassadors on earth. The primary manner in which the Kingdom advances is the preaching of the Gospel accompanied by miracles of healing and deliverance.

> *And they went out and preached everywhere, the Lord working with them and confirming the word through the accompanying signs* (Mark 16:20).

THE GLORY IS FOR BATTLE

I (Mahesh) was born and raised in Africa. I lived only about a hundred miles from Tsavo, a region made famous by two massive lions that killed 130 people over a nine-month period. The movie, *The Ghost and the Darkness,* is based on the true story of the man who tracked down and killed these lions. As a teen I hunted near Tsavo. The area was still inhabited with lions, so my friend and I always took an African guide with us. It was his job to keep fires going through the night. The light kept the lions at bay, but one time our guide fell asleep, and the fires went out! In the middle of the night, I was jolted out of sleep by a blow to the face. It felt like my jaw had been hit with a club. Shocked and trying to get my bearings, I heard a noise that sent a shudder through my bones. It was a lion roaring as he was on the prowl right outside of my tent. The blow to my face had been the flick of his powerful tail.

Lions roar into the ground, and the earth literally picks up the lion's vibration. The sound can travel for miles. The lion's roar outside of my tent shook the earth, shook my tent, shook my liver—and I had a revelation—*Lion!* My heart almost exploded— Lion! Lion! My kidneys responded, and I immediately needed a change of underwear. When a lion roars right next to you, it strikes awe and terror into every part of your being. That is what happens to the demonic realm when the Name of Jesus is proclaimed. He is the Lion of the Tribe of Judah (see Rev. 5:5). Jesus said, *"The Spirit of the Lord is upon Me...to set at liberty those who are oppressed"* (Luke 4:18).

> '[Christ] *will roar like a lion. When He roars, then His sons shall come trembling from the west; they shall come trembling like a bird from Egypt, like a dove from the land of Assyria. And I will let them dwell in their houses,' says the Lord* (Hosea 11:10-11).

Bonnie and I visited the Chicago Field Museum to see the Tsavo man-eaters on exhibit there. Because the pelts of the original lions were so bullet scarred, the two lions' proportions had to be greatly diminished to recreate a facsimile of the live ones. As we stood before the display, we thought, "Is this what everyone was so afraid of?" They didn't appear at all as terrifying as the account of death and destruction we'd heard. It reminded us of the words of Isaiah describing the fallen angel lucifer when Jesus comes in power: *"Those who see you will stare at you and ponder over you: 'Is this the man who made the earth tremble, who shook kingdoms...?'"* (Isa. 14:16 ESV).

The Lion of the Tribe of Judah is seated on the throne *"far above all rule and authority and power and dominion, and above every name that is named, not only in this age but also in the one to come"* (Eph. 1:21 ESV).

THE GLORY IS FOR VICTORY

Many people think because He is the "Prince of Peace," Jesus is a pacifist. He calls Himself a Man of War, God of angel armies, Captain of the Hosts (see Exod. 15:3; 1 Sam. 1:3 TM; Josh. 5:14). The last book of the Bible describes the great war in which Jesus is the conquering King riding out over the earth in the power of the Spirit. He is armed with a bow and wearing a crown as He goes forth *"conquering and to conquer"* (Rev. 6:2). He is the King regaled in Psalm 45:

> *Gird Your sword upon Your side, O mighty One; clothe Yourself with splendor and majesty. In Your majesty ride forth victoriously in behalf of truth, humility and righteousness; let Your right hand display awesome deeds. Let Your sharp arrows pierce the hearts of the King's enemies; let the nations fall beneath Your feet. Your throne, O God, will last forever and ever; a*

> *scepter of justice will be the scepter of Your kingdom.*
> *You love righteousness and hate wickedness; therefore*
> *God, Your God, has set You above Your companions by*
> *anointing You with the oil of joy* (Psalm 45:3-7 NIV).

He is the Lamb that was slain. He is the victorious King. The cross is the bloody testament of the violence of His battle, and the glory of His victory.

As we step beneath the shadow of the cross, He is the One anointing us for battle. The Bloodied One who was dead and is alive equips us with authority, power, and spiritual weapons for His victory in our battles. We have learned some practical things about spiritual warfare:

1. *Victory is settled, but satan hasn't conceded defeat.*

This is the tension between the "already" and the "not yet" of our victory in Christ. During Jesus' days of ministry on the earth, He sent out disciples to heal the sick, cast out demons, and work miracles. They returned exclaiming, "Even the demons are subject to us in Your name!" Jesus replied, "I saw Satan fall from heaven like lightning. Behold, I give you the authority to trample on serpents and scorpions, and over all the power of the enemy" (see Luke 10:17-19). Miracles of healing and deliverance are manifestations of the Kingdom of God on the earth. Every conversion of a sinner is a major spiritual victory.

We conduct "treasure hunts" in our ministry school. We take teams of believers to local malls to pray for people and share the Gospel. The treasures we seek are hurting hearts and lost souls. Before going out, the teams pray and seek out what the Lord quickens to them. Chad, a member of one team, was led by the Spirit into a local bookstore. He heard a young man ask the clerk for the section containing books on the supernatural. Chad followed the man and asked him what he was seeking. "A satanic bible," the man said. Chad knew this man was the treasure God was seeking that night.

Chad briefly explained that the forces of darkness are a counterfeit of true spiritual power. He shared about Christ's victory at the cross and then prayed. Chad says, "I didn't feel anything when I prayed for him. But I knew that the Lord had divinely led us to this man who was searching for truth." Later, Chad and the team were debriefing in the parking lot. As Chad shared about the encounter, the team looked up to see that very man pass in front of their car. Chad exclaimed, "That's the guy right there!" The moment Chad pointed, the man projectile vomited. That is a classic manifestation of deliverance from demons. It was a token for the team that night. They witnessed the power resident in Christians as warriors of the true light!

Christ is working today exactly as He did when He walked the earth two thousand years ago. If you have received Him, you have received His Kingdom with power and authority. We have peace with God through His blood, but He is at war with His enemies. We have been commissioned to carry His victory and loose captives from satan's grip.

Every Christian has an active commission. You are the salt of the earth. You are the light of Christ in the world. None of us is exempt from this calling. We have an anointing from the Holy One. Our assignment is for greater works. Jesus said, *"He who believes in Me, the works that I do he will do also; and greater works than these he will do, because I go to My Father"* (John 14:12).

2. *The anointing breaks the yoke! (See Isa. 10:27.)*

The anointing is the atmosphere of God's glory released. In that Presence, mighty strongholds come down. When God's people faced the formidable task of rebuilding the ruins of His Temple, God said, "It's not by might, not by power, but by My Spirit!" (see Zech. 4:6).

In spiritual warfare, we must recognize and draw on the anointing of God's Spirit resident within when we face mountains of opposition. *"It shall come to pass in that day that his burden will be taken away from your shoulder, and his yoke from your neck, and the yoke will be destroyed because of the anointing oil"* (Isa. 10:27). Prayer, fasting, praying in the Spirit, and meditating on Scripture all help reinforce and refill you with His anointing. But in the long run, it's not you or your power; it's Jesus through His Spirit who conquers the powers of darkness. You simply become His ambassador of victory in this world.

Here is the testimony of one of our students:

> One day Habakkuk 1:5 came to me out of the blue: *"Look among the nations and watch—be utterly astounded! For I will work a work in your days which you would not believe, though it were told you."* I knew it was from the Lord, and it was for me.
>
> A short time later, my father e-mailed me from England. He wanted to come for a visit. It was a complete surprise. I had not had much contact with my father since I was eight years old. He always claimed to be an atheist and believed in reincarnation. When I told him that I was going to Bible College, he laughed. In the middle of his visit, he asked me about my beliefs and I gladly shared the Gospel with him. When Sunday came, I invited him to come to church, assuming he would find a way not to go at the last minute. As we entered the church sanctuary and the service started, my father's mouth dropped open. He had never experienced anything like it.
>
> I could tell he was deeply touched. At the end of the service, I invited him to meet Pastor Mahesh. In the

next few moments, he prayed with Pastor and gave his life to the Lord.

His words were, "That Sunday morning service changed my whole life and thinking." When we got back to my apartment, we prayed together. For the first time in my life, my father blessed me in Jesus' name! Today my father is plugged into a Spirit-filled church in England where he continues to grow in the Lord.

That word from Habakkuk came to pass. If someone had told me the week before my father's visit that this would be so, I would not have believed it.

In our sanctuary, the young man's father encountered the Presence in the anointing. The glory of the Holy Spirit flowed through every person he met, resounded in every word that was spoken, and changed his heart. In the anointing, true light pierced the darkness that had held him in bondage for decades.

3. Let the Big define the Small.

One day as Mahesh was in his study, an angel of the Lord suddenly appeared and the glory exploded in the atmosphere around him. The angel had the smell of fresh battle on him; it was clear he had just come from one war and was on his way to the next. He looked at Mahesh and exclaimed, "How big is your chair?" Then the angel disappeared. In the air all around, Mahesh heard the strains of an old hymn:

> *Come, Thou almighty King,*
> *Help us Thy Name to sing,*
> *help us to praise!*
> *Father all glorious,*

> *o'er all victorious,*
> *Come and reign over us,*
> *Ancient of Days!"*[3]

Early Americans sang this song during the Revolutionary War. Hessian mercenaries once stormed a Sunday service, demanding that the congregation profess allegiance to the king of England. As the organist played the music of "God Save the King," the congregation sang words of allegiance to a different King! The soldiers, with swords drawn, looked on as the people sang:

> *Come, Thou Incarnate Word,*
> *gird on Thy mighty sword,*
> *our prayer attend!*
> *Come, and Thy people bless,*
> *and give Thy Word success,*
> *Spirit of holiness,*
> *on us descend!*
> *Come, holy Comforter,*
> *Thy sacred witness bear*
> *in this glad hour.*
> *Thou Who Almighty art,*
> *now rule in every heart,*
> *and ne'er from us depart,*
> *Spirit of power!"* [4]

We must keep a fresh revelation of God's majesty burning in our hearts. God is enthroned in the praises of His people. We give authority to that which we exalt. When we enthrone God over the battle, the limitations of the situation around us no longer define us. If we focus on the challenge, we allow the small to define the big. Focusing on little distractions saps the strength we will need for the real battles God is anointing us for. When you exalt Him, His presence comes. As you make His chair big in your heart, you release His glory. You become congruent with Him. That's the place of miracles.

Rehearse God's intervention in your life and the lives of your loved ones. Recall what He has done in the past. Enumerate His miracles. Enthrone Him in your heart, and connect with the glory of His Presence. Then turn that glory upon the opposing realms of darkness and turn the situation around.

4. *Angels warring with us.*

Angels respond when our words agree with Heaven. *"Bless the Lord, you His angels, who excel in strength, who do His word, heeding the voice of His word"* (Ps. 103:20). When Daniel read the words of Jeremiah, he realized it was time for God's promise to be fulfilled. He did not define himself according to the might of the Persian Empire. He came into agreement with God through prayer and fasting. As he harmonized, the angel Gabriel came to help. The angel said, "Your words were heard; and I have come." Daniel's prayers mustered the heavenly armies. It effected a shift in the spiritual administration over the nation and brought a mighty king to his knees in worship before Daniel's God.

Angels are spiritual beings whose bodies have no spatial limitations. Believers have the anointing of the Holy Spirit and the authority of Christ without limit. When persons whose mighty, heavenly bodies are without limit join forces with persons whose spiritual authority from Christ is without limit, they are formidable.

Angels are holy messengers sent to help His saints in battle, *"Are they not all ministering spirits sent forth to minister for those who will inherit salvation?"* (Heb. 1:14). In times of conflict, they come to our aid. Angels ministered to Jesus after He confronted satan in the wilderness. They came to strengthen Him as He prayed in Gethsemane.

Angels come to give strength for overcoming evil forces. They are here to help you in battle. Angels are sent in answer to your prayers for you, your family, your church, and your nation. Angels are sent forth as they are commanded in harmonious assignment with God's word of promise. As you wage warfare in the spirit, be aware that you can activate and loose angels in the authority of Jesus' name.

5. Sometimes the problem is people.

Spiritual conflict involves human agents in one way or another. Our biggest vulnerabilities are often connected to those we love most. Their weakness, or ours, may give the enemy a place to stir up trouble. This can devastate families, churches, businesses, and even nations. We do not wrestle against flesh and blood (see 2 Cor. 10:3). But really good people can be conscientiously committed to really bad ideas or involved in really bad things. This aligns them with the forces of darkness and it affects others. A glance at human history shows the world is full of examples of persons whose ideology or work became a force of evil. Christians are to be warriors of light. Jesus said we overcome evil with good that comes from Him. The cross is the ultimate mechanism for the defeat of satanic forces. It reconciles humanity to right relationship with God. Through the cross we love our enemies and pray for those who misuse us. Love is a powerful opponent of evil. Forgiveness is love in action. Ultimate forgiveness is the glory of God shining from the cross. There the Just One forgave the unjust. *"Make allowance for each other's faults, and forgive anyone who offends you. Remember, the Lord forgave you, so you must forgive others"* (Col. 3:13 NLT).

6. Authority is a personal relationship with Christ.

> *Then some of the itinerant Jewish exorcists took it upon themselves to call the name of the Lord Jesus over*

> *those who had evil spirits, saying, "We exorcise you by the Jesus whom Paul preaches." Also there were seven sons of Sceva, a Jewish chief priest, who did so. And the evil spirit answered and said, "Jesus I know, and Paul I know; but who are you?" Then the man in whom the evil spirit was leaped on them, overpowered them, and prevailed against them, so that they fled out of that house naked and wounded. This became known both to all Jews and Greeks dwelling in Ephesus; and fear fell on them all, and the name of the Lord Jesus was magnified* (Acts 19:13-17).

The religious experts in the story from Acts had no authority when they used Jesus' name. They didn't even know Him. They had only heard about Him. They could not wield His authority because they were not in relationship with Him. They weren't His "own." This is one of the most important spiritual principles. When you are rightly related to the Lord and in the place He has appointed you in His body, great power is released to and through you. To use Jesus' name you must know Him personally. He said:

> *All authority has been given to Me in heaven and on earth. Go therefore and make disciples of all nations, baptizing them in the name of the Father and of the Son and of the Holy Spirit, teaching them to observe all things that I have commanded you; and lo, I am with you always, even to the end of the age* (Matthew 28:18-20).

Jesus told His followers, *"From the days of John the Baptist until now the kingdom of heaven suffers violence, and the violent take it by force"* (Matt. 11:12). Overcomers must be prepared to face down persistent evil with persistent power in the anointing of the Holy Spirit. The cross was very violent. The Lord Jesus resisted and persisted until He had completely conquered His enemy. Let us take our strength from Him.

The anointing for spiritual authority flows from the top down, from Christ to us in the power of the Spirit. Jesus marveled that a Roman soldier understood the chain of power in spiritual kingdoms better than Jesus' disciples did. The Spirit of the Lord God is upon us. We are members of His supernatural army. We are messengers of light and love. Through us Jesus stretches out His hands for healing and deliverance in His name. You wield His scepter extended from His throne. Use it for His glory!

THE LIGHT OF HIS GLORY

As the Captain of Armies, the Lord has gone out to war against all opponents of His glory. He is calling up His reserves, and renewing spiritual commissions for battle. Israel carried the Ark of the Testimony whenever they went to war. The blood of atonement was sprinkled on the Mercy Seat that sat over the cover of the ark. The glory cloud rested on the blood between two mighty cherubim. The ark was the key to victory in battle. In the glory, God's power was exerted to provide for and cover people walking in agreement with Him. And in the glory, His judgment was revealed against the adversaries of righteousness. This all typifies the victory and salvation wrought by Christ through the cross and the Spirit who raised Him from the dead.

The importance placed by Israel upon the Ark of the Covenant is unsurpassed. God communicated with Moses face to face *"from between the two cherubim"* on the ark's cover (see Exod. 25:22). The ark and its sanctuary were considered *"the beauty of Israel"* (see Lam. 2:1). The ark was carried by the priests in advance of the people and their army (see Num. 4:5-6; 10:33-36; Ps. 68:1; 132:8). When the ark was borne by priests into the flooded Jordan, the water parted and a pathway opened for the entire host to pass through (see Josh. 3:15-16; 4:7-18). The city of Jericho was taken with a shout after the ark was paraded for seven days around its walls (see Josh. 6:4-20). Judgment and deliverance were in the ark. The ark was Israel's instrument of war against all enemies. When the ark was in the midst of Israel, the divine Presence was there, too. Israel had continual supernatural victory over their enemies as long as the ark was in its proper place and they were serving God in an acceptable manner.

The ark was holy and created a distinction between holy and unholy. Ultimately, the Presence with the ark meant judgment or deliverance, life or death. Every ark in the Bible, from Noah's ark to the ark that saved Moses as a baby, was an instrument of preservation during judgment. This too symbolizes Christ, our Mercy Seat in divine judgment.

The Mercy Seat covered the ark and was called "the propitiatory," picturing the propitiation for sins that would be made through Christ's blood. The High Priest sprinkled the blood on the Mercy Seat on the Day of Atonement prefiguring Christ's ascension into Heaven to make intercession for us with the offering of His blood once and for all. Two Cherubim were molded together with the Mercy Seat from one piece of pure gold. Nothing wooden, nothing human, only gold, only God, provides deliverance from sin and victory over spiritual enemies warring against man's soul. The pure gold speaks about God's person, nature, character, and purpose while the wood speaks about humanity: *"In this is love, not that we loved God, but that He loved us and sent His Son the propitiation for our sins"* (1 John 4:10).

It was there, between the Cherubim over the Mercy Seat, that God said He would meet His servant face to face:

> *And there I will meet with you, and I will speak with you from above the mercy seat, from between the two cherubim which are on the ark of the Testimony, about everything which I will give you in commandment to the children of Israel* (Exodus 25:22).

The cloud that was deliverance for Israel and darkness for her enemies, the glory that led her through the wilderness, descended to rest over the ark in the Most Holy Place. *"Oh, give ear, Shepherd of Israel, Thou who dost lead Joseph like a flock; Thou who art enthroned above the cherubim, shine forth!"* (Ps. 80:1 KJV). The cloud of God's Spirit and the mighty cherubim are present with the ark. *"The Lord reigns, let the peoples tremble; He is enthroned above the cherubim, let the earth shake!"* (Ps. 99:1)

The cloud is two-fold just as it was in the Tabernacle: one was the cloud of incense prescribed for worship and the other the responding cloud of God's glory. The cherubim are mighty armed guardians as seen in Genesis 3:24 outside the Garden of Eden with a flaming sword. They are instruments of worship and war. They face one another in agreement, their wings spread over the Mercy Seat. They demonstrate the presence of mighty hosts involved in defense of the saints and advance of God's kingdom.

The blood that makes atonement (see Rom. 5:11) gives us unbroken, full and free access to and provision from God hour by hour. It speaks with Christ's absolute authority. The Priest could not enter into the Holy of Holies where the ark was without the blood. We, too, must enter in by the blood. We have entered into the Holy of Holies where Christ rules from His throne in Heaven through us on earth. The blood and the Spirit cover and anoint us for service and equip us for battle against principalities of wickedness. Believers wage war and gain victory over powers of darkness.

Together with the saints who have gone before, you are part of a spiritual army commissioned for victory in the battle. We have been positioned as the front line of God's advance against the kingdom of darkness on the earth. We overcome by the blood of the Lamb and the word of our testimony, the testimony of Christ, the testimony of His presence and power, all greater than that seen in the testimony carried in the ark when Israel went out to war. We now have Christ Himself! The cloud of His presence is covering us. Jesus' word and His blood speak on our behalf before the Father. In the cloud He speaks to us, refreshes and anoints, and communes with us as a loving Father does His children.

WARRING IN THE GLORY

Jesus is our Ark of Covenant in which our promises reside:

> *"Having therefore, brethren, boldness to enter into the holiest by the blood of Jesus, by a new and living way, which He hath consecrated for us, through the veil, that is to say, His flesh"* (Hebrews 10:19-20 KJV).

The ark contained three powerful things: The tablets that are the authority of the word and the promises of God towards us who believe. The rod of Aaron is the anointing of the Spirit to walk in supernatural power and grace. The golden bowl of manna is God's provision for our lives day by day. The ark is command central for all spiritual battle. It contains a seven-fold supply of benefits in our lives: protection and provision; presence and power; promise and peace; all communicated as we give ourselves in service and obedience as worship to the praise of His glory.

Let us each fulfill our part of the mission. Through provision of the cross and the resurrection we have been given all we need to wage effective spiritual warfare in this life. The power of the blood and anointing of the Holy Spirit are the Ark of Christ present with us, going before us, protecting us and giving us victory in all situations for the glory of God. This equipping includes the belt of truth to strengthen our core being; the righteousness of Christ to give our hearts courage; our progress forward with peace at all times; a shield of faith over all; our minds renewed in Christ and therefore full of optimism because we have been saved (see 1 Thess. 5:8); the supernatural word of God and the unction of the Holy Spirit for a sword of defense and offense; and continual prayer in tongues and in words of human understanding! (See Eph. 6:13–18.)

We have five essential strategic weapons in the glory-arsenal at our disposal every hour. They are: the prayer of agreement to bind and loose spiritual powers (see Matt. 18:8-20); thanksgiving (see John 6:11,23;11:41); praise (see Ps. 8:2; 2 Chron. 20:21-24; Acts 16:25-26); proclamation (see Rev. 12:7-11); and the gifts of the Spirit for revelation (see 1 Cor. 12:7-11). Your first tactical move must be to identify and bind the strongman behind the stronghold you are facing (see Matt. 12:29), remembering that God has provided the necessary spiritual weapons and that you come in authority and Presence of the Ultimate Champion, Christ.

> *For though we live in the world, we do not wage war as the world does. The weapons we fight with are not the weapons of the world. On the contrary, they have divine power to demolish strongholds. We demolish arguments and every pretension that sets itself up against the knowledge of God, and we take captive every thought to make it obedient to Christ* (2 Corinthians 10:3-5 NIV).

The ark symbolized Christ our High Priest ruling from the throne of God. Christ Himself is the Mercy Seat where His blood speaks, and there, in a mystery, the Spirit of Glory abides with us as a cloud. The hosts of Heaven are sent out on behalf of the saints. In the cloud of covering as the blood speaks and our worship and praise agrees, we welcome the mighty Presence of God to go before us in every situation. As we come into agreement, we are aligned in battle ranks and decrees are loosed in Heaven and earth to the glory of God!

> *And they overcame him by the blood of the Lamb and by the word of their testimony, and they did not love their lives to the death* (Revelation 12:11).

ENDNOTES

1. From *The Dream of the Rood,* lines 57-58, 60-61, 63-69. Translation copyright © 1982, Jonathan A. Glenn. Used by permission.

2. Shirley Jackson Case, *Origins of Christian Supernaturalism* (Chicago, IL: University of Chicago Press, 1946), 1.

3. See http://library.timelesstruths.org/music/Come_Thou _Almighty_King/.

4. *Ibid.*

CHAPTER 7

WHERE IS GOD?

With dark nails they drove me through: on me
those sores are seen,
open malice-wounds....
They mocked us both, we two together.
All wet with blood I was,
poured out from that Man's side....
I saw the God of hosts
harshly stretched out. Darknesses had
wound round with clouds the corpse of the Wielder....
All creation wept,
King's fall lamented. Christ was on rood.[1]

✝ ✝ ✝ ✝ ✝ ✝ ✝ ✝ ✝ ✝ ✝ ✝ ✝ ✝

"**O**ut of darkness—light!"

I suppose that is the best way to sum up my knowledge of what He came to mean to me. It wasn't He that attracted me in the beginning. The whole region was going after Him. It was the excitement in the heat and throng of those crowds that was irresistible to me. There I could be unrecognized, at least at first. There I could win for a few moments an admiring eye of a stranger and draw him into my grasp. But what happened the day I met Him changed all of that. He changed all of me, forever.

My town lay on the western shore of the Sea. Magda was the city of boat builders and fishermen. They were a rough crowd and I should know. I came to experience the harsh embrace of my city the year my father died. My indenture for his debts meant seven years service to a fish salter. If I let my mind run back, I can still taste the sting of it on my lips. I can smell it on my hair.

That old master and his sons used me in turn. I was too frightened to do other than comply—just turned marriageable, but an orphan. I kept my fears and tears to myself once it had begun. Before long, I had other abusers. Although they did not have bodies of flesh and bone, those abusers tore me all the more.

It's gone now. All of it. All of them.

I don't hear them anymore. Their grating nails have loosed my heart. He drove them out with a glance. Where once was wild waste filling the void in my body and soul, there is joy and peace. The bitter root those rough gardeners plowed in me was uprooted in His grip of grace. There is light where darkness once overwhelmed. Now there is only beauty.

He came to our region, and I went out with the crowd. By then I suppose I was a menace and not quite in my right mind. But I had business to attend to, so I schemed that in the mill of the crowd there would be some lonely-eyed soul who would accept the invitation in my eye and in turn pay a day's wage into my purse. By the end of the night, I had money enough to feed myself for the next three. So I followed the throng that followed Him, and while He sowed, I reaped in turn, gleaning from the corners of the field that had begun to swell around Him.

I grew bolder as the days went by. On that day as everyone else answered His invitation, I whispered, as I had done before, my own invitation beside a man's ear. How was I to know the man I had my eye on was one of His. The heat and sun and dust pressed together with the murmur of those who wondered at the Rabbi's words. I waited and repeated myself twice more. I was about to slip away unanswered. Then my quarry suddenly grabbed my dress and would not let me go.

The hands laid on me this time were destiny.

While the crowd dispersed, my captor spoke.

"Let's go!"

My heart beat fast as I followed him, only to find myself shoved before the One they had all come out to see. He was my man's Master. The man I "chose" whispered to me as he thrust me into their midst.

"Behold the Lamb of God who takes away the sin of the whole world!"

I stumbled and fell before the Nazarene. As He raised me up, it was with kindness I had not known at the hands of men. It was with clear and pure eyes I had not felt on me since my father's last look when I was a child.

When His eyes pierced my heart, it was not with lust or hatred.

"Mary."

How did He know my name? He spoke once and all my tormentors left me in His presence. I don't mind at all that my story is told everywhere. He is the Deliverer of Israel. He delivered me. And I followed Him after that. Never was there love like this. Pure love. He suffered for it, and we saw Him die.

And out of darkness came light.

I believed His words and we watched through the night as Passover came. His mother slept at last, her weeping abated only after exhaustion took her over. In the distant predawn, the first cock crowed.

"Mary," I said, hating to wake her. "The hour has come."

We put on our shoes and slipped out to where they had laid Him. As we entered the garden, we found the earth upturned and graves open! Who had done this? I shuddered as we passed the press, its heavy stone and bowl a reminder of His crushing. Two women alone—who would help us open His tomb so we could dress the body for proper burial?

As we turned the corner, the gaping mouth of the cave seemed to exhale when our eyes fell on its opening. The stone was rolled away. I left His mother and ran, my bundle of spices clutched tightly to my breast. I bent inside, my heart pounding in confusion. His tomb was empty! There on the shelf the strips of linen were neatly folded as if put aside for the launderer. Sitting beside them, a young man dressed in white gazed at my stricken expression.

"What have you done with Him?" I cried.

His mother came in and saw the empty grave clothes.

"He is risen," the man told us. "Go and tell His friends. He will meet you."

At first they wouldn't believe. But I insisted, and finally, Peter and the one who first brought me to Him agreed to go and see for themselves. I stayed behind, wondering what I would do next. Where would I go? Who would I go to? Only the gardener's form lingered behind the trees. I wept unashamed.

"Mary."

I turned at the Voice—thinking at first it was the gardener, but it was Him just as He had said!

Imagine yourself in a dark room with no light sources anywhere, all dark. It is night, and there are no windows. The door is closed, and no light is seeping in under the crack of the door from the hallway. Your eyes are open, but you can't see a thing.

Now, suddenly, there is a lighted candle in the middle of the room, its flame warm and glowing. Now you can see the corners of the walls, the outline of the furnishings. From the light of one candle, you begin to make out your surroundings. You can make your way around the room without bumping into the furniture. Better yet, if you pick up the candle and hold it in front of you as you begin to traverse the room, you can see everything clearly as you extend the candle toward the object.

The cross brings everything into perspective. What seems the darkest of moments to the natural eye is the brilliant light of God's glory demonstrated.

WHILE IT IS YET DAY

Now as Jesus passed by, He saw a man who was blind from birth. And His disciples asked Him, saying, "Rabbi, who sinned, this man or his parents, that he was born blind?" Jesus answered, "Neither this man nor his parents sinned, but that the works of God should be revealed in him" (John 9:1-3).

This poor man's suffering was not a judgment. It was so that God might show forth His glory through him. Jesus continued,

"I must work the works of Him who sent Me while it is day; the night is coming when no one can work. As long as I am in the world, I am the light of the world" (John 9:4-5).

Jesus spat on the ground and made clay with His saliva; then He anointed the eyes of the blind man. *"Go, wash in the pool of Siloam"* (John 9:6-7). The blind man came back seeing. This scene calls creation to mind. The Creator steps into human history. He takes a misshapen earthen vessel in His Creator hands and remakes him in His own perfect image.

God's disposition toward human suffering is summed up in Acts 10:38: *"God anointed Jesus of Nazareth with the Holy Spirit and with power, who went about doing good and healing all who were oppressed by the devil, for God was with Him."* He is the Healer; He is the Deliverer; He came to destroy the works of darkness. Human suffering is not divine retribution. Suffering exists as a result of the entrance of sin into this world. Sin is a spiritual force that levies corruption and anguish on the human race. The cross is the answer to suffering as it is the answer to sin.

Why do good people suffer? The Bible, in the Old Testament and New, is full of human difficulty and tragedy. It's as if the mortal world occupies a shadowland between the ravages of sin and the advent of the Healer. The glory of God takes center stage and He displays His splendor most clearly against the backdrop of suffering. The cross is God's consolation and His answer to the problem of pain. He enters the suffering cosmos to become its Burden-Bearer:

> *Surely He has borne our griefs and carried our sorrows....He was wounded for our transgressions, He was bruised for our iniquities...by His stripes we are healed"* (Isaiah 53:4-5).

His advent assures us that His Day is coming when there will be no more pain, no more sorrow, nor sighing, nor tears (see Rev. 21:4).

Sometimes, religious tradition blinds men's hearts. The Pharisees protested the blind man's healing because it was done on the Sabbath and they assumed the suffering was the result of somebody's sin. Their conclusions were wrong in both cases. I (Mahesh) remember an incident while ministering in Brazil. A woman who was immobilized with pain from a horrible back condition was miraculously healed during one of our services. She had at one time been a renowned dance champion in her region. In an instant, years of terrible pain and suffering ended, and I will never forget the scene of her and her husband gloriously dancing across the room, demonstrating the miracle of God for all to see. Their daughter wept as she watched her mother move with ease, but some of the organizers of the city-wide meeting were offended that the couple were dancing in church.

Healing and miracles are God's work every day of the week. Religious tradition and religious legalism hold the human race in the very chains Jesus came to break. In Mark's Gospel, he tells of a man from Gadara who was keeping a whole region in terror. A legion of demons tormented this poor man until he was driven from his family and community and was living in a graveyard. Jesus made a special trip to set the man free. He sent the legion of oppressors into a herd of pigs. When the townspeople saw the glory of the Lord, they asked Jesus to leave (see Mark 5:1-17). There will always be people who choose pigs, even when the Lord shows His glory!

All human suffering is drawn into the cross. There God suffered in the flesh, taking sin, judgment, and ultimately death into His own body. The balm for all those who experience suffering in this world and do not find relief is the resurrection. The resurrection is the ultimate hope of glory (see Col. 1:27; 3:4). Eternal punishment will be exiled from the Presence and glory of the Lord (see 2 Thess. 1:8-10). Our comfort in the midst of tribulation is that suffering in this world is at most temporary, but our redemption, including redemption of the body, is coming! Our confidence and our hope give us assurance while we wait for the Lord: *"If we suffer, we shall also reign with Him"* (2 Tim. 2:12 KJV).

There is glory in the cross. We have consolation in Christ. The resurrection is our ultimate hope. Until then, we commune with Christ day to day. In Him we find peace. Jesus is the reason for our joy even in the face of suffering: *"In the world you will have tribulation; but be of good cheer, I have overcome the world"* (John 16:33).

GLORY IN THE MIDST OF TROUBLE

The early Church embraced tribulation in this world as fellowship with Christ and His cross. It transformed their tribulation into victory. This is a spiritual enigma. The first Christians held the idea that the Body of Christ continues to occupy space of active redemption in the earth. For them, if they suffered from persecution or infirmity, they were personally participating in Christ's intercession for the world. Paul wrote:

> *I rejoice in my sufferings for your sake, and in my flesh I am filling up what is lacking in Christ's afflictions for the sake of His body, that is, the church, of which I became a minister according to the stewardship from God that was given to me for you, to make the word of God fully known, the mystery hidden for ages and generations but now revealed to His saints* (Colossians 1:24-26 ESV).

We hardly understand this. How can anything be lacking in Christ's afflictions for the sake of His Body? Yet His first disciples understood this and rejoiced in suffering *for the sake of His glory* even when it cost them their lives. They embraced the opposition, tribulation, and suffering as part of their prophetic mission.

> *To them God chose to make known how great among the Gentiles are the riches of the glory of this mystery, which is Christ in you, the hope of glory. Him we proclaim, warning everyone and teaching everyone with all wisdom, that we may present everyone mature in Christ. For this I toil, struggling with all His energy that He powerfully works within me* (Colossians 1:27-29 ESV).

What made them so different was Christ's presence empowering them within the world. Christ was not an escape clause or their warranty against trouble. They took their strength from the cross during times of tribulation. So must we.

The work of Calvary is spiritual, but it affects every aspect of our lives. First, we are regenerated; born again; made members of Christ's eternal glorious body. Secondly, Calvary is provision for our soul—intellect, will, and emotion. The blood exchange provides power for access by the Holy Spirit and for God's word to change us into His likeness. Thirdly, the cross is healing for our bodies as by His stripes we were healed (see Isa. 53:5). Through His body offered, our bodies are set apart as His dwelling place. The Spirit in us will raise us up in the resurrection—a glorious spiritual body in place of this natural decaying one (see 1 Cor. 15:49). Fourthly, the suffering of Christ on the cross provides spiritual fellowship for comfort when we suffer because we live in spiritual hope.

The proposition that the glory of God breaks out in the midst of trouble is a bold theme in spiritual history. It is one which brings strength and help in time of need. Paradoxically, with God, weakness permits power, death leads to life, and victory comes out of suffering. Christian suffering will bear fruit of overwhelming happiness when Christ appears (see 1 Pet. 4:13). It makes us partakers in the same glory Christ possesses (see 1 Pet. 5:1). Suffering is temporary, but glory is eternal (see 1 Pet. 5:4,10). Testing is part of "suffering" as is persecution for righteousness' sake. Testing, and we do not mean a temptation to sin but discipline from the Lord, in times of difficulty exposes our weakness to His strength and makes us more like Jesus. This is *"a mystery, the hidden wisdom which God ordained before the ages for our glory..."* (1 Cor. 2:7). In Scripture, a mystery is not an enigma, but rather truth that has been hidden and is now revealed. Hidden wisdom does not remain hidden. The cross is the wisdom of God. The cross is on display.

NIGHT AND DAY

The *White Crucifixion* is a painting by Marc Chagall that depicts Christ, wrapped only in a Jewish prayer shawl, suffering on the cross. All around Him are images of Jewish suffering: the pogroms of Russia; Jewish families fleeing, hiding from their persecutors; a mob bearing weapons overrunning Jewish houses and setting them afire; villagers seeking to flee aboard a crowded boat; an old man wiping tears from his eyes; another clutching a Torah, looking back at his synagogue in flames. No one passing through those dark nights would dare suggest it was not "great tribulation."

Chagall's painting seems to groan. At its center is the cross, its suffering rabbi a member of every Jewish family. He is not removed from their torture, grief, rejection, and loss. And in those scenes there is another Sufferer, too. Perhaps they see Him. Perhaps they are remembering another Jew who was cast out. Perhaps they may remember a once-told story of a Son of Judah. One who came among them claiming it was He they were waiting for. Has He entered into His suffering or have they entered into His? Either way the two are in communion. The Rabbi and His people. They share the fellowship of suffering. They are one.

Now let us pause a moment and think about our world. Like Chagall's painting, the whole world groans under the weight of human suffering that lays on it. It challenges our perception of redemptive victory. What happens in the gap between words of faith and devastating circumstances we encounter in the world? There is not a family anywhere that has not, does not, or will not experience suffering of one kind or another, at one time or another. We all share in it. Trouble comes like a blast of dry heat from a desert. We could easily despair. That is where the glory of the cross enters into our darkness. There He is. His bloodied arms stretch out to us in understanding and strength. He bids us to receive His embrace. He offered

Himself through the Spirit for the sake of the Father. When suffering comes, let us do the same. Through obedience, even passion unto death, He strode toward the cross. We meet Him there. His cross becomes ours, too. We enter fellowship with Him there. His heart firm and His face set, He anticipated great joy that awaited Him on the other side of suffering. Glory was being gathered from the folds of deepest gloom. He and His Father, They and Their Companion Comforter went down into the valley of shadows. Hosea says the Valley of Trouble is our door of hope. A song comes up from the crevices of that valley. A song of knowing Him as He is. A song of revelation of His love for each of us. It's a first-love song.

> *"Therefore, behold, I will allure her, Will bring her into the wilderness, And speak comfort to her. I will give her her vineyards from there, And the Valley of Achor as a door of hope; She shall sing there, As in the days of her youth, As in the day when she came up from the land of Egypt. "And it shall be, in that day,"* Says the Lord, *"That you will call Me 'My Husband...'* (Hosea 2:14-16a).

Let's take another look through the lens of Scripture and the writings of a Jew who knew that Calvary casts a different light on the darkness humans experience in the course of life in this world. He wrote,

> [We are] *heirs of God and fellow heirs with Christ, provided we suffer with Him in order that we may also be glorified with Him. For I consider that the sufferings of this present time are not worth comparing with the glory that is to be revealed to us* (Romans 8:17-18 ESV).

The Sabbath fell between Calvary and the resurrection. It seems there is a pause between suffering and glory. Hebrews encourages us to *"strive to enter* [His] *rest"* (Heb. 4:11 ESV). Jesus rested in the middle of the storm on the Sea of Galilee. He rested when He fulfilled the words of the psalmist, *"Into Your hand I commit My spirit"* (Ps. 31:5). We rest, even in times of trouble, because we are partakers of His finished work. We have hope and faith toward things not seen, allowing His Word to surround us with His glory and the cross to provide us power. In his book, *The Cross of Christ*, John Stott concludes:

> The cross transforms everything. It gives us a new worshiping relationship to God, a new balanced understanding of ourselves, a new incentive to give ourselves in mission, a new love for our enemies, and a new courage to face the perplexities of suffering.[2]

RESURRECTION POWER

The apostle Peter proclaimed:

> *Men of Israel, listen to these words: Jesus the Nazarene, a man attested to you by God with miracles and wonders and signs which God performed through Him in your midst, just as you yourselves know—this Man, delivered over by the predetermined plan and foreknowledge of God, you nailed to a cross by the hands of godless men and put Him to death. But God raised Him up again, putting an end to the agony of death, since it was impossible for Him to be held in its power* (Acts 2:22-24 NASB).

The Greek word translated as "agony" is the word for the labor pains of childbirth. When the Holy Spirit raised Jesus from the dead, God put an end to the birth pangs of death. The tomb became the womb for a glorious new creation! When the devil tells you, "It's over," it's the beginning of something glorious. The tomb is a womb for your breakthrough!

We are to put on Christ. The first promise in your promise box is probably not, *"In the world you will have tribulation"* (John 16:33), but Jesus gave this warning to console and prepare His disciples to overcome the world. The Holy Spirit is the Comforter. He is in us and with us, and He is with us in our trials. In the same way that a woman's labor pains ultimately deliver the much anticipated baby—our trials produce the image of Christ who is being formed in us. Jesus' story does not end in the tomb, nor does ours. *"Now Christ is risen from the dead, and has become the firstfruits of those who have fallen asleep"* (1 Cor. 15:20). Through the cross of testing, just on the other side, is glory. Eternal Easter day is dawning in the resurrection. Until then, we carry the power of that resurrection within us and let it out in miracles when we pray.

The greatest miracles will occur in the face of the greatest darkness. Early in my (Mahesh's) ministry, my spiritual mentor, Derek Prince, and I were holding evangelistic outreaches and ministry training in Pakistan, one of the darkest regions I have ever visited. Spiritually and physically, the oppression and literal filth, suffering, and disease were present everywhere. Most people lived in abject poverty. Even in our Western hotel, electricity was intermittent, and bathroom facilities were almost nonexistent. And if, as I found one night, you needed to use the open sewer that served as the hotel bathroom in the middle of the night, it gave the Scripture, "Whatever you have to do, do it quickly!" a whole new meaning. When I stepped into the bathroom, something crunched under my feet. I turned on my flashlight, and there all around me were thousands of roaches.

The bathroom floor was a carpet of roaches! They were climbing up my legs. Aahhhh! The spiritual atmosphere of the region, steeped in generations of idolatry and witchcraft, was not much different than the horror of that nighttime bathroom experience.

Every day, on our way to the open air field where we held our meetings, Derek and I passed by an elderly blind woman who sat begging on the road we traveled. One day, Derek asked me to stop and take a picture of the woman. Born without eyeballs, seated in the filth of the street, she was representative to us of the spiritual and physical darkness that engulfed this region so desperately in need of the light of Christ.

Later that night during the healing service, I sensed God's glory was in the meeting for a great deliverance. I took authority over the powers of darkness that held the region in bondage. There was a loud clap of thunder, and it seemed I heard all the demons screaming as I declared the name of Jesus, the King of Glory. There were literally tens of thousands of people in the meeting. But, out of the crowd, a lone woman came forward. She was wearing the same sari as the woman that I had photographed earlier in the day. She testified to the whole crowd, "You know me. I am blind all these years, and this man prayed; I saw a flash of light, and now I can see." Where there had been no eyes, she now had dark brown, beautiful eyes that shone with the joy and light of the One who came to snatch her out of deep darkness. The opening of her physical eyes resulted in the opening of the eyes of her heart, and thousands of others who witnessed the event, giving them a life of joy in the midst of those ongoing, terrible circumstances. Her photograph and story are in my book, *Only Love Can Make a Miracle.*

TRANSFORMING EVERYTHING

The resurrection power that came through the cross creates everything anew. It also transforms our perspective on suffering. The miracles we have seen testify to the glory of God and His great goodness as He intervenes to relieve despair and suffering in the human condition. We rejoice in every miracle, both small and great, and we long to see them at every turn. Miracles are given to confirm God's message. Jesus said, "Believe Me for the works that I do" (see John 10:38;14:11). He meant that the miracles demonstrated the truth of His proclamation.

Miracles are for glory. Miracles often take place center stage in the midst of suffering. The crowd in the wilderness could have gone hungry for the half-day journey back to food, but the loaves and fishes witnessed to more glory. Jesus wept with Lazarus' sisters even as He was the glory of resurrection to come. Lazarus' death was much more than the loss of a brother to his two sisters. His resurrection returned their family's provider. But it also stirred up Jesus' enemies who sought to kill Lazarus because of his testimony!

I (Bonnie) remember the day that our son Aaron was undergoing his fifth surgery. Following a devastating pregnancy where both our lives had been in grave danger, Aaron was born at just twenty-five weeks after conception. Our baby had multiple physical and congenital life-threatening challenges and was given only days to live. Mahesh was in Africa, as I had insisted that he keep a prior commitment to hold evangelistic outreaches in Zambia and Zaire. Following months of physical trial in my own body and the strain of a second son being born with complications that were far worse than what we had experienced with Ben, I had a moment of resentment and self-pity. In my angst I exited the waiting room of the hospital. The sky was gray with rain, and I stood under the portico leaning on one of the pillars feeling sorry for myself. My internal voice said, "Lord, if this is the way You treat your friends..." In that very moment, the eyes of my spirit were opened, and I saw Jesus standing in a mirror image of my own, leaning against the other side of the pillar. He said, "Bonnie, I am here. That is more than enough for all you need." His voice was the voice of the Comforter. Our battle for Aaron lasted three years, but every day, in every situation, Jesus was present to heal. Today Aaron is in graduate school, perfectly whole physically, mentally, and spiritually.

The night Aaron was born the Lord appeared to me in a dream and gave me Psalm 29:8-9:

> *The voice of the Lord shakes the wilderness; the Lord shakes the Wilderness of Kadesh. The voice of the Lord makes the deer give birth, and strips the forests bare; and in His temple everyone says, "Glory!"*

Sometimes God seems to hide for a season. The year before Aaron was born, I (Mahesh) held the dead body of a mother's child in Zambia. Though the boy was not resurrected when I prayed, I saw the glory of God when his mother, a new believer, with tear-filled eyes confidently told me, "He can no longer come to me, but one day I will go to him." She was trusting in the power of the cross and the glory of resurrection. The next year I went back to that region, and at the very time our son Aaron was suffering on the threshold of death, God resurrected six-year-old Katshinyi Manikai when I prayed for him in Zaire.

> *Is anyone among you suffering? Let him pray. Is anyone cheerful? Let him sing psalms. Is anyone among you sick? Let him call for the elders of the church, and let*

them pray over him, anointing him with oil in the name of the Lord (James 5:13-14).

We have been in the business of praying for and witnessing miracles for most of our lifetimes. We can no more cause a miracle or explain why they do or do not occur today than at the time we saw the very first one. But we believe. And we see them. We pray for miracles every time. No matter what, we still believe and worship. There are no formulas, there is only Him. His glory is revealed even in the face of darkness.

Through Darkness Into Light

Dietrich Bonhoeffer had already made a mark through his writings and scholarship at the outset of World War II. While a pacifist, Christ called him to become an active intercessor in the clash between light and darkness as Hitler arose and Germany's destiny hung in the balance. At first Bonhoeffer escaped. He wrote to a friend, "I have made a mistake in coming to America. I must live through this difficult period in our national history with the Christian people of Germany. I will have no right to participate in the reconstruction of Christian life in Germany after the war if I do not share the trials of this time with my people."[3] He went back to Germany and took an active role in plotting Hitler's death. Bonhoeffer was ultimately arrested, imprisoned, tortured, and hung by the Third Reich. He wrote in *The Cost of Discipleship*:

> To endure the cross is not a tragedy; it is the suffering which is the fruit of an exclusive allegiance to Jesus Christ. When it comes, it is not an accident, but a necessity. It is not the sort of suffering which

is inseparable from this mortal life, but the suffering which is an essential part of the specifically Christian life.... The cross is there, right from the beginning, he has only got to pick it up; there is no need for him deliberately to go out and look for a cross for himself, no need for him deliberately to run after suffering...[4]

Bonhoeffer lived the life he wrote about—the life of a disciple. He embraced the cross in the midst of darkness and became a shining light. He wrote:

The first Christ-suffering which every man must experience is the call to abandon the attachments of this world. It is that dying of the old man which is the result of his encounter with Christ. As we embark upon discipleship, we surrender ourselves to Christ in union with His death—we give over our lives to death. Thus it begins; the cross is not the terrible end to an otherwise God-fearing and happy life, but it meets us at the beginning of our communion with Christ. When Christ calls a man, He bids him come and die....Every day he encounters new temptations, and every day he must suffer anew for Jesus Christ's sake. The wounds and scars he receives in the fray are living tokens of this participation in the cross of his Lord.[5]

The physician witnessing his execution said, "I have hardly ever seen a man die so completely submissive to the will of God."[6] His last words spoken to fellow prisoners as he was taken away were, "This is the end—for me the beginning of life."[7]

Our dear friend Leslyn was diagnosed with Stage IIIc cancer when she began to have a series of dreams. The Holy Spirit began comforting and instructing her for the intense challenges she would face. Leslyn's experience is a powerful example of our personal participation in the power of the cross in the midst of suffering.

> The first few dreams I had, I was dressed in a white linen shift that came just below my knees, and I was running along a beach. I was running in a way that only people in really good shape can run—fast, unfettered, and full of joy. I was never tired, and I could feel the wind in my face and hair.

> About the third dream in this series, I was running as before, but this time I came to a place where a high wall of rocks jutted out into the water, cutting off the beach completely. I could go no further and had to stop.

> The next night I was again at the rock wall and began to walk along the face of the rock as it veered into the water. I then saw the smallest glimmer of light coming from the rock, and I realized that there was a break in the rock that went into a cave. The light was the tiniest prick of light coming from far away at the other end of the tunnel. I then noticed that the opening in the rock was the exact shape of my silhouette without my breasts or my hair. I realized that the only way for me to get through this rock face was to be in the very condition in which I found myself following my surgery and cancer treatments.

> This was very encouraging for me, because deep down in the recesses of my heart, I had secretly wondered

if my cancer was the result of some failure on my part. Perhaps I had not prayed or warred enough in my life. But this dream laid to rest those worries and concerns that somehow I was not in God's will or had failed. It was all settled in a moment when I saw that opening in the rock in my dream. I knew this was the path that I was to walk. The Holy Spirit let me know that God did not cause my cancer, but this trial would take me to a place that I could not get to in any other way, and that it is really true that all things work together for the good of those that love Him.

I stepped into the opening of the rock, but I had to slide in sideways. The space fit me perfectly. I then began to shimmy through the tunnel. The space was so tight that I had to hold my arms perpendicular to my body and slowly inch my way along sideways. This journey through the tunnel continued for quite awhile; in every dream, I inched a little bit farther toward the light. I realized after several of these dreams that the way I had to move through this tight space was by walking in the shape of the cross.

In the year following my diagnosis, I got closer and closer to the end of the tunnel and began to catch glimpses of a beach that I had never seen before at the other end. I knew that that was my destination as soon as I passed through this rock. As this book goes to print, I am happy to report that this series of dreams ended when I had a vision while I was worshiping at our church. I saw myself stepping into brilliant light onto that beach. At the very moment I was experiencing this

> vision, other people observed a visible light surrounding me all around. I am doing much better now, regaining my strength and expectantly walking into a new day.

This year has been really tough, but this dream gave me a bigger picture that helped me know that I was making progress, and that God's hand was sovereignly moving in my life even in the midst of this trial. As I was passing through the Rock of Christ, His Presence and His assurance gave me phenomenal peace even as I experienced deep personal challenges and physical transformation in the process. In the dark, I was hidden there in the cleft of His Rock, and through the cross I am experiencing His glory.

In all of this, Leslyn never lost her joy. Happiness comes from circumstances, but joy comes from God. *"You make known to me the path of life; in Your presence there is fullness of joy; at Your right hand are pleasures forevermore"* (Ps. 16:11 ESV). Christ endured the cross for the joy of pleasing the Father, of bringing many sons to glory and of the reunion and Kingdom that was coming. But the suffering of God did not end at the cross. We suffer with Him and He with us in the fellowship of His Body. Faith is the victory that overcomes the world.

It is particularly in times of suffering that Calvary becomes most dear to us. There is no other answer sufficient to the question of human suffering except the knowledge that Christ suffered also. He suffered for glory. Let our suffering be the same example to the world. Everyone who embraces the call to sonship must join with the Son in the cross. No death, no resurrection. No cross, no glory.

> *The Spirit Himself bears witness with our spirit that we are children of God, and if children, then heirs— heirs of God and fellow heirs with Christ, provided we*

suffer with Him in order that we may also be glori-
fied with Him. For I consider that the sufferings of
this present time are not worth comparing with the
glory that is to be revealed to us. For the creation waits
with eager longing for the revealing of the sons of God
(Romans 8:16-19 ESV).

HOUR OF POWER

The glory of the cross is multidimensional. It is substitutionary, regenerative, and triumphant. It accomplishes the sanctification of men, the satisfaction of God, and the destruction of evil. Seven times in the Gospels Jesus calls His passion and crucifixion as "the hour" for which He came (see John 12:23-33). The cross released power through the life in His blood. The blood releases the power of the Spirit to raise the dead. The power demonstrated is revealed again and again in the word. We experience the power of God, the power of salvation, the power of the Spirit, the power of the Kingdom, the power of Christ, the power of prayer, the power of deliverance, the power of preaching the word, the power of the Gospel. The power of the cross!

In his commentary on Colossians, John Eadie says:

Our redemption is a work at once of price and power—of expiation and of conquest. On the cross was
the purchase made, and on the cross was the victory
gained. The blood that wipes out the sentence against
us was there shed, and the death which was the death-
blow of Satan's kingdom was there endured.[8]

The apostle Paul walked in Christ's glory. Paul took up the cross as he embraced his calling and followed in the steps of Christ. Through his self-giving, the Gospel spread abroad. The renunciation of self through suffering gave way to great power through the Gospel:

> *I now rejoice in my sufferings for you, and fill up in my flesh what is lacking in the afflictions of Christ, for the sake of His body, which is the church, of which I became a minister according to the stewardship from God which was given to me for you, to fulfill the word of God, the mystery which has been hidden from ages and from generations, but now has been revealed to His saints. To them God willed to make known what are the riches of the glory of this mystery among the Gentiles: which is Christ in you, the hope of glory. Him we preach, warning every man and teaching every man in all wisdom, that we may present every man perfect in Christ Jesus. To this end I also labor, striving according to His working which works in me mightily* (Colossians 1:24-29).

Five times, Paul received thirty-nine lashes. He was stoned, shipwrecked, snake-bitten, imprisoned, naked, and in peril. Yet he said "I am the least of the apostles" and "the chief of sinners" (see 1 Cor. 15:9; 1 Tim. 1:15). He spent fourteen years in the desert, worked for his own support, submitted to others in spiritual authority, cast out demons, and healed the sick. And once, when suffering himself, he prayed three times for relief. When the word came back, "My grace is sufficient for you," Paul left it at that and got about his business in the Kingdom! Let us do the same.

ENDNOTES

1. From *The Dream of the Rood,* lines 46-47, 48-49, 51-53, 55-56. Translation copyright © 1982, Jonathan A. Glenn. Used by permission.

2. John R.W. Stott, *The Cross of Christ* (Downers Grove, IL: InterVarsity Press, 1986), 11.

3. Eberhard Bethge, *Dietrich Bonhoeffer: A Biography* (Minneapolis, MN: Augsburg Fortress, 2000), 655.

4. Dietrich Bonhoeffer, *The Cost of Discipleship,* trans. R.H. Fuller (New York, NY: Touchstone, 1995), 88-89.

5. *Ibid.,* 89-90.

6. Eberhard Bethge, *Dietrich Bonhoeffer: A Biography* (Minneapolis, MN: Augsburg Fortress, 2000), 927.

7. *Ibid.,* 928.

8. John Eadie, *A Commentary on the Text of the Epistle of Paul to the Colossians.* 2nd ed., Edited by W. Young. (Edinburgh: T&T Clark, 1884), 169.

CHAPTER 8

AWAKENED IN GLORY

*He then rose to heaven. Again sets out hither
into this Middle-Earth, seeking mankind
on Doomsday, the Lord himself,
Almighty God, and with him his angels....
He asks before multitudes where that one is
who for God's name would gladly taste
bitter death, as before he on beam did....
Nor need there then any be most afraid
who ere in his breast bears finest of beacons;
but through that rood shall each soul
from the earth-way enter the kingdom,
who with the Wielder thinks yet to dwell.*[1]

✝ ✝ ✝ ✝ ✝ ✝ ✝ ✝ ✝ ✝ ✝ ✝ ✝ ✝ ✝

He came right through the wall. Like the Strongman He is. Like the Owner of the place. Like the parables He always told us. We were clueless of what He meant until He showed up. He broke into the very place we had run to hide. He walked right in and ransacked our hiding place. Ran out all our fear and unbelief. Especially mine. Purely ransacked our souls with the intention of chasing out every shadow of a doubt.

Oh yeah, I'm *that* guy. The one who is famous for one pitiful thing: not believing Him. It wasn't that I didn't believe *in* Him—I knew He was Messiah alright. There was no doubt about that. I knew *that* from the start. Believing *Him* is a whole different story. At least it was for me. Difference between night and day. The difference between what we saw when they killed Him and what we saw when He stood smack-dab in our midst on glory day.

He really is the Beginning and the End. Not just of a time, a thing, even a person's own existence. He is the original Original. The Source of absolutely all, down to the last detail. Like they say, "It's not over till it's over." Believe me, He's not over! Yes, some of this world we live in has been corrupted, given itself over to darkness. So what? He is the light. So get on with it! That's the other thing I learned.

He said, "On the third day I will rise again." If He said it once, He said it a hundred times, and yet we couldn't believe He would be crucified. And apparently we never even got to part two—that He would live again right after. And moreover, live *in* us. Some of our womenfolk, though, they were fanatics start to finish. Like His mother and Mary. They grieved in inconsolable horror, and so did we, for what He went through. We watched the whole ordeal, standing there on the hill, Passover fully upon us. But those women believed. Believed Him through and through. Deep down, they knew it wasn't really over. That's why they were the only ones to go out to the tomb in the morning. The ones who saw Him before the rest of us. The first ones to carry back the good news that He isn't dead. And I do mean *isn't*. He's not past tense. That's what I found out the day He broke in.

So let me tell you about glory day. The day I broke out of the past—left the old me behind and hit the right-here-right-now-forever full on! We were all there in the room, nerves on edge and pretty depressed after what had happened. Never mind that the guys who ran the show up at the Temple already hated us. Word was spreading like wildfire that we were history, too—toast. They were looking for us everywhere. So we hid out. We laugh at ourselves from where we sit now. Like we really could have stayed under cover. Or like *He* couldn't find us!

One minute it was all doom and gloom and the next minute I was standing up in front of Him like, "What the hey? Is that You, Jesus?" My mind in a whirl and my body suddenly on fire from top to bottom, inside out, like the furnace of Shadrach, there He was. I fell into Him weeping in awe and relief—and in disbelief! Put yourself in our shoes, or at least in mine—I mean, *I really loved Him, and I saw what they did*. Believe me, it's a scene that only His showing up as He really is could take away. And so excuse me if I seemed a little slow on the uptake— look at the rest of my life. You'll see that I got with the program, got on the bandwagon. The power of His resurrection...*You know what that means?!*

Once you've experienced Him as He is, you just can't go back to before. I saw it time and again. The power of His resurrection flowing right out of my own hands. Coming through the ones He stretched out to me in the room. He said, "Here, Tom, grab hold. See? That's where the nail went in and you fell down cursing my executioners. Well, here I AM." As though those hands became alive inside my own. I was convinced and I became a convincer. He said that too, remember? "Anyone who believes in Me, the works that I do...and greater works...he will do also." It's not a question. It's the facts.

All I ever wanted was to just get where He was going. Be where He is. Be like Him. We went everywhere together after that. The power and proof like a living river rushing out of us all, bringing life back to desert souls everywhere. We all went in different directions. North, south. Hebrews, goyim. That was the whole idea. His idea from the beginning—but man, does it take awhile for the light bulb to come on sometimes! Folks tend to get set in their ways, you know?

See, my brother and I—we were twins—we were always those kind of down-in-the mouth guys. Sort of had a tendency to *examine everything.* We'd accept nothing on pure face value. I liked to look a horse in the mouth, if you know what I mean. But there's a limit to just how far that will take a guy. See, in my mind I was so committed to Him, that when He said He was going to die, I just threw up my hands and said, "All right then. I guess we're all in this together." Exactly. But I was missing the point. We are in it to live, not die!

His death means we live—and live to tell about it. We're walking provers that He's not dead and that He's still making stuff happen through us while we're here. Just like Him. People used to say my brother and I were look-a-likes. Walked and talked like each other. Couldn't tell one from the other. But I'll tell you who I'm really like. There are a lot of stories. People want to know. Did I go to India? Hey, what difference does it make? And do you really need to know how I died? I laid myself down in Him. The point is that *just like Him, I am alive!* You will be too, if you believe.

And by the way, that whole thing about carrying my supposed bones all over the place—maybe I could understand it if my bones had done what Elisha's had! I'm laughing here. It's all true what He said. It's all real what He did. And just like He told that criminal who *deserved* what *he* got, "Today is your day for glory!" That's the power of His resurrection. Everything we did after that day when He broke in on us, that day He brought us out of the old mind-set and set us upon the world to bring His deliverance to the rest, I mean every single thing we did after that flowed out of glory day! Heal the sick, cleanse the lepers, cast out devils, *raise the dead*. Whoa! That's the full package to the possessors, the new strongmen. You know what they call us now? *Believers*! Don't see Him? Just believe Him. And believe me,

He'll show up. I know what I'm talking about. Do the stuff. He lives!

A few years ago at Easter, our church put on a traditional Sunday morning drama. In it Christ was to emerge from His "tomb" and announce His victory over sin and death forever. Unfortunately, as the drama unfolded, there was a slight hiccup behind the scenes.

Having successfully reenacted a bloody, suffering Christ who gave up the ghost and was taken down from the cross by caring friends, our Jesus was whisked away, quickly washed down backstage, re-dressed in white, and installed into the backside of his tomb. He waited for his cue to appear in glory. But the director got ahead of himself and sent Jesus out before the songs anticipating his appearing had ended. The other actors and the audience were surprised to see him in his "resurrection."

A confused look was on the "savior's" face as he emerged and the audience gave a collective gasp. But, being quick on his feet, our Jesus quickly realized he had been given the wrong cue. He shrugged and ducked back into his tomb. As he disappeared, a voice was heard from the audience, "I guess this means six more weeks of winter!"

EYEWITNESS ACCOUNT

Fortunately for all of us, there were no missed cues or second thoughts when the real Jesus came out of the grave on resurrection morning! More than five hundred people saw, spoke to, walked with, and ate with Jesus after He emerged alive from the tomb. The winter of sin and death was vanquished forever. The glory of His resurrection is experienced in small foretastes as we walk in communion with the Spirit who raised Jesus up. The consummation of this glory will come when we are raised up to be with the Lord on the last day.

In His death, Jesus sealed off the entire corrupted heritage of Adam together with its sentence of death. Christ became the Last Adam when He came in a body of flesh. He became the Second Man, the Progenitor of the new race, in His Resurrection. On the cross, Jesus declared the words that were said by the High Priest when the sin offering was made in the Tabernacle: "It is finished!" These words meant atonement for trespass had been accomplished. The sin that had separated the people from their God was taken out of the way. Christ paid the penalty in full on behalf of every man, woman, and child ever born. He took into His own body the sum and consequences of the first Adam's failure.

> *For since by man came death, by Man also came the resurrection of the dead. For as in Adam all die, even so in Christ all shall be made alive* (1 Corinthians 15:21-22).

Jesus is the Last Adam. He legally usurped the failed works of the first Adam. And so, He fathered a new race of sons for God. We have been born again, not of the flesh or the will of man, but of the Spirit according to the pleasure of the Father.

The Holy Spirit descends and remains on the Lamb. The glory rests on the ark. The blood of covenant and the glory of God commune together. It's a great mystery. We are Christ's Body. We are the "called out ones." We are destined for glory. We are becoming His glory.

We cannot know Father without knowing Son. We cannot know Christ, except the Spirit reveals Him to our hearts and minds. Each of us finds our full identity in Christ as we are integrated into the community of saints, our local church.

This is the rock on which I will put together My church, a church so expansive with energy that not even the gates of hell will be able to keep it out (Matthew 16:18 TM).

Jesus was declaring that no power on earth or under the earth can withstand His Kingdom. His Body manifests His Kingdom in a *corporate* way. The Body of Christ speaks of interdependence and a chain of command, permanent relationships, practical service, and love. It speaks of authority and dominion flowing down from the Head to touch the earth.

Heaven and Earth Together

The origination of God's relationship to man is the cross. In His death Jesus closed the chasm between the human race and God. In His resurrection Jesus filled us with the Spirit of His glory. The Holy Spirit is our Person-to-person connection to the Father. Jesus is the Mediator. *"For there is one God and one Mediator between God and men, the Man Christ Jesus"* (1 Tim. 2:5). Christ stands between you and everything else; between you and everyone else. He even stands between the "old man" and the new creation in you. There is no room for anything but Christ to come between us and the world, between ourselves, between us and ourselves! Christ stands between. The cross and the Spirit make our fellowship with God and others possible.

The Holy Spirit is the Resident Lord of the Church. The Spirit binds us together in a body. He is continually building up Christ's Body in the way a master sculptor brings a masterpiece out of a block of clay. Our spiritual construction will continue until we become *"a perfect man"* in the fullness of the stature of Christ (see Eph. 4:12-13). The end purpose is God's glory, strength for the body, and a glorious Bride for Christ.

Jesus told His disciples, *"Nevertheless I tell you the truth. It is to your advantage that I go away; for if I do not go away, the Helper will not come to you; but if I depart, I will send Him to you"* (John 16:7). This is the fullness of Christ. This is the glory of the Son, the manifold wisdom of God, made visible to principalities and powers through the Church (see Eph. 3:10).

Bonhoeffer speaks to this in *The Cost of Discipleship:*

> The Body of Christ takes up space on earth. That is a consequence of the Incarnation. Christ came into His own. But at His birth they gave Him a manger, for "there was not room in the inn." At His death they thrust Him out, and His Body hung between earth and heaven on the gallows. But despite all this, the Incarnation does involve a claim to a space of its own on earth. Anything which claims space is visible. Hence the Body of Christ can only be a visible Body, or else it is not a Body at all...A truth, a doctrine, or a religion need no space for themselves. They are disembodied entities. They are heard, learnt, and apprehended, and that is all. But the incarnate Son of God needs not only ears or hearts, but living men who will follow Him.[2]

Jesus said, "You are the salt of the earth." Salt disinfects, preserves, and binds together. The Body of Christ is present in the earth as a cleansing, preserving presence against sin and its wounds upon humanity. The Church occupies space in the earth as salt and light. We are the demonstration and proof that Jesus Christ is alive and working today.

> *You are the light of the world. A city set on a hill cannot be hidden. Nor do people light a lamp and put*

it under a basket, but on a stand, and it gives light to all in the house. In the same way, let your light shine before others, so that they may see your good works and give glory to your Father who is in heaven (Matthew 5:14-16).

We are the light of the world. We are not carriers of the light. We are not professors of the light—we *are* the light of the world as He is. We are to shine forth with the brightness of His glory. His body cannot be hidden. It is a company of believers in communion with Him and with one another. His body is a visible, tangible extension of the Head Himself.

Dating from the birth of the Church at Pentecost, we see Christians participating in ongoing activity, fellowship, and communion with one another. Their existence is never to be a "me and Jesus" only affair. The blueprint for the Church of Jesus is sketched out in the Book of Acts:

They continued steadily learning the teaching of the apostles, and joined in their fellowship, in the breaking of bread, and in prayer. Everyone felt a deep sense of awe, while many miracles and signs took place through the apostles. Day after day they met by common consent in the Temple; they broke bread together in their homes, sharing meals with simple joy. They praised God continually and all the people respected them. Every day the Lord added to their number those who were finding salvation (Acts 2:42-47 JB Phillips NT).

Here we see a corporate manifestation of Christ in a many-membered order, showing forth God's glory on the earth. We see a vibrant community awakening in glory. As many members of one body, they are caring, loving, helping, encouraging, and blessing one another. As the Head of His Body, Christ directs and nourishes the Church and makes Himself visible to the whole world.

There are seven pictures of the Church in the Book of Ephesians. These seven expressions include: assembly, body, workmanship, family, temple, bride, and army. Each of them is corporate. Each of them is visible. Each of them occupies space. Each of them has structure by which that expression exists and fulfills its function.

A body has a proper structure when it's healthy. A house is built according to a blueprint. To govern effectively, a legislative assembly observes protocols. You cannot have community without order. You cannot have order without structure. You cannot have structure without authority.

The glory makes a distinction between God-appointed and self-appointed leaders (see Num. 16:20-35,41-45). Glory is bound up in God's leader's lives as though He claims their reputation for His own (see 2 Sam. 1:17-19). In Exodus 16, the glory came to mediate truth and judgment when the people rebelled against God's appointed leaders. Moses interceded, asking God to pardon. God relented, but He promised that all men would see His righteous judgment: *"I have pardoned, according to your word. But truly, as I live, all the earth shall be filled with the glory of the Lord"* (Num. 14:20-21 ESV). This event prefigures Jesus interceding for us and the glory of God demonstrating mercy and judgment through the cross.

As we honor our leaders and honor each other, we reflect the Godhead. Disciples of Christ are the *"glory and joy"* of those who teach them (see 1 Thess. 2:20). The Lord meets us in fellowship and His glory appears.

And above all things have fervent love for one another, for 'love will cover a multitude of sins.' Be hospitable to one another without grumbling. As each one has received a gift, minister it to one another, as good stewards of the manifold grace of God (1 Peter 4:8-10).

It is essential now more than ever that Christians live in vital interaction with God and one another through participation, worship, sharing the sacraments, learning, growing, and serving together in ongoing fellowship within a visible church community.

GLORY IN THE FAMILY

Jesus' priority is to reconcile us to those who are also reconciled to God as He brings us each into His family. Family is the essential building block of human society. In the same way, the covenant community is the geographic location for coming home to God and His family. In the local church we find God in Person, and God in *persons*. There we discover the fullness of our own spiritual identity in a way that isolation from this community can never actualize. The local church is central command for God's advancing mission.

As the Lord of glory is on display in the midst of His people, His power to transform lives is present. Here is a glory story:

> *Melanie:* I grew up in a Christian home, so through all my life I had a knowledge of the need of salvation. However, I did not have a knowledge of the Holy Spirit or of a personal relationship with the Lord, so there was a gaping hole inside of me that issued an open invitation to be filled by something. Unfortunately, for twelve years, that something was darkness. In college, I turned my back on the Church and entered the gay lifestyle.

After years of this life, I was invited to a Glory Conference by my sister, who had recently come back to the Lord. I was afraid, but hungry at the same time, so I went. As soon as the worship started, my mocking and fearful heart encountered a Presence of a Person, and everything that was in disagreement with the Lord of glory had to bow.

Then, Pastor Mahesh Chavda came to the pulpit and declared, "Let the King of Glory...*Come In!*" Instantly, I heard the sound of huge steel doors slamming shut one after another all around me, and the Lord said to me, "I have closed the doors of your past, and I am sealing them shut." I was freed from the gay lifestyle and also got a fresh start in every aspect of my life. I was instantly reconciled with my family and began to remember the dreams God had once given me. When I encountered the glory, my identity was restored. In the weeks following my deliverance, if the doors were open at the church, I was there!

Over the next few years, I got connected to my church family. One of the dreams Lord restored to me was to be married and have a family. One Christmas, I prayed, "Lord, by Christmas next year, I want to have my husband."

Michael: In those months that Melanie was intensely praying for her husband, the Lord began to draw me back to Himself. I was entrapped in a homosexual lifestyle that I never thought I could leave. Looking back, I can see God's hand even in my darkest hour planting seeds of His glory. I began reading my Bible and praying in the Spirit.

One night I was awakened, and the Lord said, "Choose you this day whom you will serve." I went to my living room, and the Holy Spirit began taking me to Scripture after Scripture on deliverance. I said to the Lord, "I choose You," and instantly I knew, "This is over." I was delivered, and my life began to change overnight.

While the door to my freedom opened in the solitude of my living room, the glory I experienced within the context of my church family is where I found my true identity. The Holy Spirit called to my spirit, bringing restoration and transformation.

I had come home to the Father. He reshaped my warped experience of fatherhood and reset my experience of love and relationships through His family on earth—the Church. The Church was a crucial part of deliverance for both Melanie and me.

Melanie: I was hungry for His glory. His glory kept me, calibrated me, formed, and shaped my identity into His image. My church family became the tool the Lord used to reform my "inner man." As I served, related to them, and showed up when the church family got together, I was being transformed.

Michael: A few months after coming to the church, I saw Melanie for the first time. I was sitting in home group when she walked in the door, and I heard, "That's the one!" A few weeks later, Melanie asked for prayer because she was going to share her testimony with a group of people. I was amazed when I discovered her testimony was that of coming out of the gay lifestyle! One of the things that I had asked the Lord for was a wife who had also been delivered from homosexuality.

The next opportunity, I told Melanie, "We've got to talk." We became friends, and the rest is history. Today we are married, totally in love and growing in glory together. There is nothing impossible with our God.

As Michael and Melanie came to the light of His presence they found their true identity. And they found one another. Their ongoing testimony in the midst of our church community demonstrates the power of the cross and the Presence of the Spirit that makes us whole.

THE GLORY OF MAN

Jesus purchased the Church to create a Bride for Himself. He designed the rest of creation with her in mind. Sin did not make Jesus come to earth. He came for love. His act of redemption puts the love He had before there was a world, or any sin, on display. He left His Father's side to seek a Bride: *"For this reason shall a man leave his father and his mother and cleave to his wife, and they shall become one flesh"* (Gen. 2:24). Perhaps more than any other passage in Scripture, this one proclaims the Bridegroom's intention. The only way for Him to proceed was to love us as Himself and show it in a worthy manner. He cannot deny Himself: *"For no one ever hated his own flesh, but nourishes and cherishes it, just as the Lord does the church"* (Eph. 5:29 ESV).

We are His family, but more. We are His Body, and then some. We are those in whom Christ dwells in intimate communion by the

Spirit. In us, the world sees His hands, His face, His body. Jesus said, *"He who has seen Me has seen the Father"* (John 14:9), and tells the world, "If you see My Church, you see Me."

The glory finds repose where the blood of Jesus is recognized as living and active. The intricate communion between the cross and the glory is ongoing. The blood gives the Spirit access. As the Holy Spirit resides as Lord in the Church, He is the Servant of Father and Son. He is washing our feet! This is beyond comprehension. It is as though Jesus has wrapped Himself in His Spirit as a holy towel and basin from which He is ministering to each of us continually. It is a wonderful picture of the spiritual reality provided moment by moment by the Spirit through the blood.

The demeanor of Christ is the demeanor of the Holy Spirit. And that is why we should be able to recognize the same demeanor in all who claim to be His servants. That should be so everywhere you find His disciples and even more when you are with those who are considered spiritually great. He is still serving and He is the Greatest among us. The washing power of His blood is fresh and powerful. And He is Present washing us by His Spirit and His word. The blood and the glory are at work transforming us into His glory.

GLORY IN THE CHURCH

The Shepherd of the sheep is gathering His flock. He is discipling us individually to fit together corporately. He wants us to hear His voice, not just on our own, but as His harmonious Body. He is placing us in a spiritual family in local church congregations, with established spiritual leadership. If you have not found your place, His Body has a dislocated joint and is hurting!

For your sake and His, find your place in the Body. Get into the spiritual family God has ordained for you. Fit in there and begin to contribute, serve, and grow. Don't miss out on the joy. The time of the Lone Ranger is over. God is taking away our masks and shooting our horses. This is the season to come together as His shining city. John Stott observes:

> "The very purpose of His self-giving on the cross was not just to save isolated individuals, and so perpetuate their loneliness, but to create a new community whose members would belong to Him, love one another and eagerly serve the world."[3]

The next level of glory is the restoration of the sanctity and harmony of the local church family. Each one needs the other and every joint must yield a supply of the Spirit until the whole body is built up. *Together* we will manifest the fullness of Christ. The Church is designed as a body fit together with every person rooted and producing fruit.

If you continually wander from place to place, your spiritual root system will shrivel up. In order for a plant to bear fruit, it has to stay in one place where it is tended properly. The New Testament is almost entirely addressed to specific communities of leaders as they gather together in an ongoing celebration of Christ. The Lord wants to lead us *together* and teach us *together,* and build us up *together.*

> *...whoever speaks, as one who speaks oracles of God; whoever serves, as one who serves by the strength that God supplies—in order that in everything God may be glorified through Jesus Christ. To Him belong glory and dominion forever and ever* (1 Peter 4:11 ESV).

Much work remains to be done. Harvest is at hand. The Lord of the Harvest is looking for His reapers.

Say not ye, There are yet four months, and then cometh
harvest? behold, I say unto you, Lift up your eyes, and
look on the fields; for they are white already to harvest
(John 4:35 KJV).

Let the reapers prepare. Let the harvesters go forth!

Glorious Dwelling Place

The Body of Christ is a habitation, a perpetual dwelling place
where God is literally present. He is standing in our midst. He demonstrates the glory of His Person as we harmonize in fellowship and
service.

In view of the spectacular manifestations of the glory that have
occurred in mobile church ministries, including our own, you would
think that we should look for signs of His presence *outside* the local
church. But God didn't intend for that glory just to be manifest in
the mobile church ministries. He intends to have a permanent water-
ing well, a home-hearth fire burning with the glory of His presence
where people can know to come and find the Christ they seek.

In the New Testament, the mobile ministry was rooted
in the local church. Local and mobile ministry should relationally be connected in such a way that each strengthens the
other. Too often in contemporary church culture, mobile ministry draws strength from the local expression disproportion-
ately to what it supplies. Ideally the local church creates mobile
ministry and mobile ministry builds the local church. The
dual expression should be eagerly symbiotic and never para-
sitic or competitive. Anything short of that is not Christ. The
Holy Spirit is not the author of confusion. *"For God is not the*
author of confusion but of peace, as in all the churches of the saints"
(1 Cor. 14:33).

The cross is a picture of two essential truths. The vertical beam is man's relationship with God. The horizontal beam is man's relationship with man. You cannot fully experience one without the other. Invariably, either relationship will cost us. We will have to make a sacrifice of self. This is what it means to take up the call of Christ. *"If anyone desires to come after Me, let him deny himself, and take up his cross, and follow Me"* (Matt. 16:24). The Church that is rooted and grounded, living and loving, worshiping and serving out of the fullness of the Holy Spirit is the center of God's activity on earth. There we come to the intersection of glory. It's where God and man make a family which functions together and advances as an army with banners.

> *But thanks be to God, who in Christ always leads us in triumphal procession, and through us spreads the fragrance of the knowledge of him everywhere* (2 Corinthians 2:14 ESV).

Communion means common unity. Community without order is chaos. You cannot have communion without community. You cannot have community without communion. Jesus said, *"By this all will know that you are My disciples, if you have love for one another"* (John 13:35). Communion comes out of community. Our testimony to the world is love for one another. Not love for Christ or even love for sinners. This means that we must come to a personal realization of the practical nature of the cross in our lives in community among Jesus' other kids. The cross transforms everything. It creates a community in celebration where the glory comes down!

Several years ago, we were gathered with about one thousand people in a large tent where we used to hold our conferences and weekly services. I (Mahesh) had just come up to the podium when the Lord gave me a song. I started to sing from 2 Corinthians 3:17, *"Where the Spirit of the Lord is there is Liberty, Liberty, Liberty..."* The Lord's presence was there singing over the congregation, and I just picked up His tune and began to sing along. Within a few moments I heard a collective gasp and saw a ripple of excitement rush through the crowd. People were looking up at the ceiling, pointing in awe and wonder. Because of the bright lights, I was not able to see what was happening, but I could tell *something* was happening!

I came down off of the platform and looked up to see swirling clouds of golden particles. The brilliant flecks filled the entire top of the tent, dancing in the atmosphere of glory. The glorious cloud went through the roof of the tent and was visible hovering over the roof even as we saw it manifest inside. I was supposed to bring the message that night, but when a cloudy pillar appears what else do you say? *He* was there. We stood in awe and wonder, worshiping our King. He was visiting us with His manifest presence, as we sang a corporate anthem to our Resident Lord, the Holy Spirit, *"Where the Spirit of the Lord is, there is liberty."*

As Head of His Church, Jesus sends the great Maestro, the Holy Spirit, to order and beautify His Bride. This is your time to join in His symphony. It's time to find your place in this heavenly band. We are following the cloud of His glory. He is moving to His permanent resting place and we are turning our attention toward home.

LESS OF SELF, FULLY SELF

You will always be a member of the family that you were born into, even if your relationships and natural circumstances may change. In ancient Israel, God called a family a household. A household might have as few as fifteen members or as many as three or four hundred as in the case of Abraham (see Gen. 14:14). But every family had a father. Every household had its head. Each tribe had their elders from whom they took their identity.

In the contemporary church, we think of a household as consisting of one person, one couple, or a parent and a child. And we tend to think of each household as an entity separate in identity unto itself. God's definition is different. He doesn't view His body as scattered individuals being saved and equipped with spiritual gifts for personal identity or self-edification. That's contradictory to His nature and essence of being. Even He is a community with Himself!

We are invited into the community of God and those who know Him. We have cut covenant with Christ through His blood. The gift we bring is ourselves: *"I beseech you therefore, brethren, by the mercies of God, that you present your bodies a living sacrifice, holy, acceptable to God, which is your reasonable service"* (Rom. 12:1).

No one lives unto himself alone (see Rom. 14:7). In the revelation of the blood covenant, individual salvation is directly linked to the whole household of faith. In the first Passover, God saved Israel out of slavery by households. At Jericho, He saved Rahab's whole household. When Cornelius believed the Gospel, his whole house was saved. God works with whole households.

The effect of sin is loss of community. It breaks communion with God and we find ourselves outside the garden of His delight as Adam and Eve did in the beginning. But as we come together in the Church and take up our cross, daily we share in true fellowship. The community provides liberty through interdependence. Christian liberty is liberation from the tyranny of self. In the household of God, we live beyond self-interest. We live unto one another, sharing with one another and rejoicing and sorrowing together as members of Christ. Within ongoing, permanent, believing relationships, we discover the holy treasure hidden in the people God has put around us. We discover Christ hidden in our fellow believers.

Community life is abundant life. Persons communing together speak harmonious words to one another from their hearts. Heart issues are life issues. Your physical heart is the source of life in your body. But your lungs must be in agreement. Your blood and your breath mix together to feed the rest of your self. Your blood and your breath go forth and return to your organs working in conjunction and harmony with one another. If one or the other decides to do something else, your whole body is endangered. Ultimately, your life would stop.

Abundant life is not lived in isolation. *"A man who isolates himself seeks his own desire; he rages against all wise judgment"* (Prov. 18:1). If we are always withdrawing, moving from one spiritual connection to a new one, it may be an indication of self-interest. We may be seeking self-satisfaction by seeking more of ourselves, more for ourselves. But that is never the way of the Savior of the Body. To possess and live abundant life can only mean less of self, more of others, more of Christ, more of His Spirit, more God, more glory.

The life of God by which man lives is dependent on harmony between the blood of Jesus and the life of His Spirit. If you want to see God's glory, get to know His blood. If you commune with Him through His blood, you will experience His glory. When you come into His glory, you discover it's the blood that makes the way.

In His redeemed community, our joy is made full. The little flock gathered under the shadow of the cross is the shining city set on a hill. The weary, thirsty traveler and those in need of the Healer are drawn to its light. As they enter those gates, they come home to the Father of Glory.

ENDNOTES

1. From *The Dream of the Rood,* lines 103-106, 112-114, 117-121. Translation copyright © 1982, Jonathan A. Glenn. Used by permission.

2. Dietrich Bonhoeffer, *The Cost of Discipleship,* trans. R.H. Fuller (New York: Touchstone, 1995), 248.

3. John R.W. Stott, *The Cross of Christ* (Downers Grove, IL: InterVarsity, 1986), 255.

CHAPTER 9

ISRAEL, MY GLORY

He loosed us and life gave,
a heavenly home. Hope was renewed
with glory and gladness to those who there burning endured.
That Son was victory-fast in that great venture,
with might and good-speed, when he with many,
vast host of souls, came to God's kingdom,
One-Wielder Almighty: bliss to the angels
and all the saints—those who in heaven
dwelt long in glory—when their Wielder came,
Almighty God, where his homeland was.[1]

† † † † † † † † † † † † †

He would not leave Me. This I knew. But how the body of My flesh denied it once. In council of old it was determined, to purchase again sons for God and bring them up from the grave—Israel, My glory. For this reason I had come. Gone now through shock and the beatings, beyond the jagged edge of the beam that clawed the open flesh upon My back.

Beyond the pain from spike-plowed tendons, nails piercing between My bones in hands and feet, or Roman hammers drowning out snarling priests and their company so blind. A veil fell fast on them as it fell on Me, and for a time they could not recognize that it was I who had redeemed them. I was He who kept His word to Abraham My friend.

Shema Israel! Embrace your Son. One for many.

In the din, a pure mother gasped as if she were dying with Me, and but a remnant of those who knew Me as *I Am* remained. Darkness rose and the powers of hell surrounded Me with their gaping mouths and hungry eyes. No gravity of earth, the mass that dragged Me down. Like a ship, My body was a vessel going under for the last time, and sin, My cargo. I took it under with Me. My flesh hung there suspended as a love gift, Golgotha as My altar. I had come at His good pleasure. I was His propitiation made. An offering, a sweet smell of evening incense, rising while My Father breathed Me in.

The Spirit wept, and I was handed over. Soldiers' hammers pounded out the sentence beat by beat. Divine Perfection's sledge. Justice being done as life for life I gave, the Lamb for His house. Scapegoat for His nation.

> *O My only God! Now am I abandoned, left in the straits! The waters overwhelm, and My body is going under with none to rescue. My God, My God! Why have you forsaken Me?*

A passive mass, this weight of trespass, treachery, ignorance, and death hung on Me while the storm raged. My Galilee crossing, but I didn't skip upon those waves. The error of every son from the dawn of human time until time's setting poured into Me by the entrance to the city. My body was city's temple now, destroyed. Taking in stride a rebel's death, the sentence was nailed above the One who would be King. Then darkness fell at noon, and I would become their light. When the storm had passed, I rose with healing in My wing.

Israel, My first love, though you did not know Me then, when pressed in primal mud I struggled to the finish. It was you I carried. They gave Me sour wine, and I refused. Through crimson-bloodied vision, your form like trees swaying, those I loved gripped one another with arms like branches reaching for Me though rejected by the crowd. John wept. Mary wailed and clung. Peter's loud silence followed as I descended. There could be none to rescue. I would not summon angels.

I have come to do My Father's will. With My last breath He'll hear David's evening prayer as I lay down, and it is done! Receive My soul, My Father! Into Your hands do I commit a Son for sons!

No backward glance for how they left Me, an animal corpse, suspended between the two who still resisted. Death circled as they hung there, a growling lion hungry for his prey. I was free but was not finished. Down in the distance, behind Sheol's doors all locked and barred, the old ones waited in their chains. With eyes like doves—expecting, watching at the gates where they were held. Abraham, Moses, Joshua, David, and all their sons and daughters stood together on the brink.

When they saw Me from afar, they knew that it was Me. A shout like a shofar sounded out. Their rising voice shook those gates like reeds before the wind. From Moriah and the Red Sea, from the plain at Jericho, in the pact we had cut before, many days ago. Joy pressed the dungeon doors. Hell could not separate us. Hope became sight and like a flood, a riot busted loose. And we all marched out together. My captive ones and I. All My desire and the Strong Right Arm they had waited for had come at last. Completely true to every promise I came for all who died in faith. Israel, My glory for you I came.

Lift up your heads O you gates, and lift up ancient bars! He comes! Our King of Glory in blood-drenched battle dress! His covenant remembered. Many waters cannot quench love. Even floods can't drown it! Love is strong as death, and I am jealous. No grave can shut Me in.

It was not judgment's nails I grasped then, not bars, but keys I held. I had Death by his thirsty throat. The last gasp would be his. The last laugh belonged to Me. I looked him in the eye and laughed as Hell's bars broke. Its roiling magma shuddered, exploding, and then it gave them up. They were free at last. If their loss were My gain, what would their redemption be but life back from the dead?

More powerful than up from Egypt. More glorious than out of Babylon. I carried them on eagle's wings. Their land purchased, the balance paid, a pageant of triumph in a satisfying display of splendor. No more waiting. No more longing. No more crying. No more sighing! In My arms they flew, we kings together, we brothers soaring up and up, every one in ecstasy back to the Father's place. From eternity to eternity we rose as I heard His Voice. Preceding His embrace, the Spirit breathed in Me again the breath of Heaven.

Arise, My Love, My perfect One, and come away—winter is past. The rain is gone, and the spring time of our love has come at last. Awake!

And I awoke. The tomb glistened. My radiant garment clothed Me. The stone was rolled away and angels all attended. From there to eternity I was returning. Taking the seat of My inheritance. My original chair, the place I was enthroned. Beside Me, at My right hand, came Israel, My glory!

✝ ✝ ✝ ✝ ✝ ✝ ✝ ✝ ✝ ✝ ✝

Jerusalem is mentioned by name at least seven hundred times in the Bible. That fact, plus the fact that the Jews have persisted as a people in spite of all past and present threats, is like a divine "yes" on the nation of Israel and on their capital city, Jerusalem. The God of Glory loves Jerusalem.

Through His prophets, God has promised: *"I...will be a wall of fire all around her, and I will be the glory in her midst"* (Zech. 2:5).

Through Isaiah, He declared, *"For My name's sake I will defer My anger, and for My praise I will restrain it from you, so that I do not cut you off....I will not give My glory to another"* (Isa. 48:9,11). He calls Himself the Glory of Israel: *"And also the Glory of Israel will not lie or have regret, for he is not a man, that he should have regret"* (1 Sam. 15:29).

Glory is found by those who seek God and brings rejoicing to the heart (see 1 Chron. 16:10). David, a man with a heart after God, seemed to have understood the glory. In fifty of his Psalms, glory is extolled. It is referred to as the revelation of God's Person, goodness, and power. And the psalmist says the Lord is David's glory and strength (see Psalm 3:3; 89:17-18). The Lord is the King of Glory unto whom the gates of the whole earth pay homage (see Psalms 24). Ezekiel sees the glory while he is in exile in Babylon. From there the glory begins its march home toward Jerusalem. It bespeaks the return of the people of Israel to the land that God promised Abraham (see Ezek. 1:11). That land and its people are called the glory of God (see Hab. 2:16). God's glory centers on Israel. The God of glory calls the Jews "My people" and has done so ever since the day He told Pharaoh, *"Let My people go"* (Exod. 5:1).

SIX-DAY WAR MIRACLES

The year that the Lord told us to start the Watch of the Lord, the two of us made a visit to Israel. We were staying at a kibbutz where we met and talked with a retired IDF (Israel Defense Forces) officer who had served during the Six-Day War in 1967.

He recounted to us his experience as a soldier on the front line in Sinai. Vastly outnumbered by the invading Egyptian forces, he and his fellow soldiers expected to be overtaken by the superior Egyptian army in a matter of minutes. Instead, they watched in shock as the Egyptian tank commander simply surrendered to their small force on the second day of the war. They were baffled. Why had an entire column of tanks surrendered to a few Israeli tanks?

Upon being interviewed, the Egyptian commander reported that he had seen a giant figure wielding a sword in the midst of the sand dunes where their tanks were traveling. In terror, the commander had surrendered to the IDF. This was just one of many accounts of supernatural intervention we have read or heard firsthand. This conflict ended with the recapture and reunification of Jerusalem under Jewish control.

Gershom Saloman was the benefactor of one of these miracles, and his story was reported by the news media. His uniform got caught on one of the tanks of his unit, and he was dragged and run over by the moving vehicle, resulting in a severe spinal injury. As the Syrians overtook the position where he lay, they began shooting all of the wounded soldiers. He was next. Suddenly all of the Syrians dropped their weapons and fled. Later the Syrian troops reported to the UN that they had seen thousands of angels surrounding the wounded soldier, which is why they had run away in terror.

The IDF had predicted their bloodiest fighting and losses in taking the key city of Shechem (now known as Nablus). The Jordanian army had fortified the approaches to the city with heavy artillery and tanks, so the IDF decided to circle around and fight their way into the city from the less-fortified side. Colonel Uri Banari, who led the attack, describes what happened next:

> At the entrance to Shechem stood thousands of Arabs who waved white handkerchiefs and clapped their hands. In our naiveté, we returned greetings and smiles. We entered the town and wondered: We are advancing, and there is no disorder, no panic; the local armed guards stand by with rifles in their hands keeping order, and the crowds are cheering.

Expecting reinforcements from Iraq, the entire city had welcomed the Israeli division with open arms. It was not until the forces were in the city and began to disarm the Jordanian guards that the city realized its error. This was not the Iraqi army, but the Israeli forces. It was too late, and the IDF was able to take the city.[2]

As the glorious conclusion of another miraculous battle, the Western Wall was restored to Israel. This was the place where the Temple had been, the place where the shekinah, the glory, had appeared thousands of years earlier in response to the sacrifices offered:

> *When Solomon had finished praying, fire came down from heaven and consumed the burnt offering and the sacrifices; and the glory of the Lord filled the temple. And the priests could not enter the house of the Lord, because the glory of the Lord had filled the Lord's house* (2 Chronicles 7:1-2).

From the evidence, both past and present, supported by one Scripture after another, we must conclude that the God of Glory has centered His attention on a particular, embattled people in a strife-torn land. If we are to dwell with Him in glory, the things that are important to Him must become important to us. *"Thus says the Lord God: 'This is Jerusalem; I've set her in the midst of the nations and the countries all around her'"* (Ezek. 5:5).

God hallowed Israel and Jerusalem when He sent His Son to be born and die there, and yet that does not mean that His interest is only historical. In fact, His focus on this small geographical location is intense to this day.

ISRAEL—THE CENTER OF THE WORLD

Israel is a compass for every other nation. Israel's destiny has been set according to an eternal promise God made to Abraham. Every other nation's destiny is determined by their relationship to Israel. The center of this destiny is Jerusalem, the center of the world, the apple of God's eye, the capital of the one place on earth God calls, "My land."

Many important revelations in Scripture begin or end at Jerusalem. When the first family began their journey into human history, they were headed west toward Jerusalem. God spoke to Adam and Eve. He spoke to Cain. He spoke to Enoch and Noah. Then God spoke to Abram: "Leave your father's house and go to a country which I will show you" (see Gen. 12:1). Abram obeyed, and God said, "I will give this land to you and your descendants forever" (see Gen. 12:7). God was marking out His personal property on the earth.

One step at a time, God led Abram and Sarai to the place their families would spring from. His settler was the man God called His friend. God told him, "Your descendants will be like the sand of the seashore and through your seed all the families of the earth will be blessed" (see Gen. 22:17-18). Abram was a sojourner, dwelling in tents in the land that was covenanted to him. As God dealt with Abram and Sarai, He changed them. The change was confirmed when He gave them each a new name, "Father of Many Nations" and "Princess."

On the top of the Temple Mount just behind the Western Wall in the city of Jerusalem sits a huge rock. Built around that rock is a mosque called the Dome of the Rock. Encircling the interior of that golden dome are the words "God has no son. God has no companions or has any need of them." These are words from the Koran. The rock around which the mosque was constructed is held by all three Abrahamic faiths to be the place God tested Abraham. God said,

> *"Take now your son, your only son Isaac, whom you love, and go to the land of Moriah, and offer him there as a burnt offering on one of the mountains of which I shall tell you"* (Genesis 22:2).

That rock is the spot where God provided a ram as sacrifice in exchange for Isaac. It's at the top of a range of mountains called Moriah, the "Mountain of Seeing."

There Abraham pitched his tent, defeated kings, and paid tithes to Melchizedek. There Jacob laid down and dreamed. When he awoke he saw the glory and said, "How awesome is this place! It is surely the gate of heaven!" (see Gen. 28:17). Jacob saw the future city, shining in its glory, its ministers going up and down into its Temple. He called the place Bethel, the House of God. There David bought the threshing floor from Araunah and stopped the plague that was killing thousands of Israelites. When the Holy Spirit gave David the blueprints for God's house, that ground is the place he would build it. Solomon's Temple was completed and consecrated with blood sacrifices on that mountain. That's where the glory of the Lord appeared, and He filled the house with Himself. When God moved in, the ministers and worshipers all fell down under the weight and awe of His presence (see 2 Chron. 7:1-3).

The Temple was a type of the Jerusalem to come which God is building for Himself out of persons, living stones, each containing a portion of His radiance. The Temple that God gave the Jewish people was a glorious upgrade from the wilderness Tabernacle. It was the resting place of the shekinah—that literal Presence of God manifest to the eye and entered into in intimate communion by those who seek and find Him. If you visit Jerusalem today, the ancient remains of the Temple are a center of pilgrimage, prayer, and commerce, much as in Jesus' time. On walls as you go down to the Kotel, the Western Wall of the Temple remains, the signs say, "The Divine Presence has never departed."

Just over the rampart of massive stones is the spot that God showed Abraham, Jacob, and David. Turn in any direction on the top of that Mount, and you will see the locations where the events that shape the beginning and end of man's journey occurred. Important things still happen there. For many people it's the beginning or end of a journey to find God. Moments down the road is Jesus' birthplace on earth, Bethlehem, the House of Bread, as He said, *"I am the bread of life"* (John 6:48).

Within sight are the places where Jesus shed His blood from first to last: Gethsemane; His trial at Caiaphas' house; His abuse by Roman soldiers; His passage down the street that led outside the city where He carried His cross to the place they hung Him on a tree and He poured out His blood for salvation for all. Nearby is a garden with a rich man's tomb and a nave around which is built an ancient church, all on the hill of Moriah. In any tradition, and in the ancient Greek historical records, this is the place the man Jesus of Nazareth was executed. This is the bedrock of Christian faith. Jerusalem, the city of His blood, the city of His glory.

HE'S COMING AGAIN

When the disciples stood on the outskirts of Jerusalem watching Jesus ascend into the sky, an angel appeared to them and said,

> *"Men of Galilee, why do you stand gazing up into heaven? This same Jesus, who was taken up from you into heaven, will so come in like manner as you saw Him go into heaven"* (Acts 1:11).

From that statement, supported by countless prophetic Scriptures, believers have concluded that Jesus is going to return someday, and that His Second Coming will occur at Jerusalem. Not only is the nation of Israel chosen by God (see Ps. 33:12), and not only was the city of Jerusalem the site of Jesus' first coming, but also Jerusalem is central to the restoration of His Kingdom glory on the earth.

The angel stated a promise from God, and God's promises are always powerful and consistent. Consider God's promise regarding Israel to the patriarch Abraham: *"The Lord appeared to Abram and said, 'To your descendants I will give this land'"* (Gen. 12:7). In Genesis 13:15, the Lord amplifies it, promising, *"for all the land which you see I give to you and your descendants forever."*

The promise of God for Israel and the Jewish people still stand. He said through the prophet Amos: *"I will plant them in their land, and no longer shall they be pulled up from the land I have given them"* (Amos 9:15). He is re-gathering the tribes of natural Israel and bringing them back from the ends of the earth to dwell in the midst of Jerusalem just as He has said (see Zech. 8:7-8). Furthermore, the Lord intends to make one new man of Jew and Gentile.

> *It is too small a thing that You should be My Servant to raise up the tribes of Jacob, and to restore the preserved ones of Israel; I will also give You as a light to the Gentiles, that You should be My salvation to the ends of the earth* (Isaiah 49:6).

We will meet our Savior in Jerusalem when He comes on clouds in power. John the Revelator describes the glory that culminates in the New Jerusalem where the Lamb is the ark and glory is the light of the city. In all of these occurrences, God reveals His glory as the means of announcing His triumph over His enemies. The glory is victory on parade, always leading forth in a pageant of virtue. The nations will walk in the light of His glory. And they will all bring their glory to the Lord in the New Jerusalem:

> *And I saw no temple in the city, for its temple is the Lord God the Almighty and the Lamb. And the city has no need of sun or moon to shine on it, for the glory of God gives it light, and its lamp is the Lamb. By its light will the nations walk, and the kings of the earth will bring their glory into it* (Revelation 21:22-24 ESV).

The whole world will see Him when He comes to fetch His Bride. The revealing of Christ's Bride and their marriage celebration will make the nations be overjoyed: *"Let us rejoice and exult and give him the glory, for the marriage of the Lamb has come, and his Bride has made herself ready"* (Rev. 19:7 ESV).

We have entered a covenant of blood. This glory is for us and for our children. His blood draws us into intimate communion in the cloud of His Spirit. The Glory of Christ is for us to enjoy. As we are filled with His glory, we can experience joy that is inexpressible. Jew and Gentile will sit down together with the Father and reign over the earth in glory. When He comes, Jerusalem will remain the center of the world.

PRAY FOR THE PEACE OF JERUSALEM

One of God's ageless directives is a very simple one: *"Pray for the peace of Jerusalem"* (Ps. 122:6). As we become yokefellows with the Lord Jesus Christ, He gives us a related assignment:

I have set watchmen on your walls, O Jerusalem; They shall never hold their peace day or night. You who make mention of the Lord, do not keep silent, and give Him no rest till He establishes and till He makes Jerusalem a praise in the earth (Isaiah 62:6-7).

The Lord stations watchmen on the walls to pray for Jerusalem, for Zion, for Israel, for the Kingdom of God to be established, and for His glory once again to fill the earth. Those who pray for the peace of Jerusalem will not only secure blessings for that land, but they themselves will prosper: *"May they prosper who love you"* (Ps. 122:6b).

A unique blessing comes to those who will bless the Jews. God said to Abraham, the Father of Israel, *"I will bless those who bless you"* (Gen. 12:3). His blessing is multifaceted, comparable to a banquet. At a Thanksgiving table, you have turkey and dressing and fresh rolls and great vegetables. At the end, you have pumpkin pie. You cannot come to the table and say, "I just came for the pumpkin pie." No, you come for the whole feast.

In the same way, we need to learn of every benefit that God has reserved for us. Healing is one. The breaking of family curses is another one. Cleansing of the mind is another. The presence of the glory of God comes with benefits, and, believe it or not, one key to unlock those blessings is simply praying for the peace of Jerusalem and blessing the Jewish people.

God bestows so many blessings on us that His glory shines through us. This enables us to spread the blessing to others. Not long ago, I (Mahesh) was in a restaurant in Jerusalem, and an Arab gentleman came up. He had been helping to set up the tables and clean them. He was a gentle, gracious man in his forties. He walked up to me and said, "I've met you, haven't I?"

I said, "I don't come often to Jerusalem, so I don't think I've met you."

He said, "Oh I know—television."[3] His English wasn't very good, but I could understand him. He said, "You're on the spiritual channel, and I watch you every week." Then he said, "In here [touching his chest], I saw a picture of you." I realized he was trying to say he'd had a vision. He said, "God showed me you have a big heart, a pure heart, a heart of gold. You were on a big mountain, and you had robes, and there was a gold light around you." And he started crying.

I knew God had brought me there to bless him. Then the Lord gave me a vision and a word of knowledge about his family and a specific need they had for breakthrough. I told him that God wanted them to get a breakthrough in that area. He cried some more.

I am always glad to be in Jerusalem, but I was especially glad that day to be lifting Jesus up. *"If I am lifted up from the earth, will draw all peoples to Myself"* (John 12:32).

KINGDOM OF PRIESTS

"Who is like Your people Israel, the one nation on the earth whom God went to redeem for Himself as a people?" (1 Chron. 17:21). He didn't visit and redeem the people of Indonesia or Argentina or Germany or Russia, but He decided to redeem for Himself one nation on earth, Israel, to make for Himself a name by great and awesome deeds. And, by extension, He decided to redeem all who would call on the name of the Messiah, Jesus.

In the Bible, *Israel* appears two thousand five hundred times. By virtue of sheer repetition, if for no other reason, we must believe that God has given Israel a special status, to the point that we cannot understand His will at all unless we understand His intentions for the Jewish people. In the New Testament alone, Israel is mentioned seventy-nine times. *Jew* is mentioned eighty-four times in the Old Testament and a hundred and ninety-two times in the New Testament. In contrast, *Christian* is mentioned only three times in the Bible. It's something to think about. By paying attention to what God emphasizes in His word, the names that have been so often repeated, you will gain insight into your own promised-land provision.

Jesus said, *"Salvation is of the Jews"* (John 4:22). He said that because He Himself was a Jew and because without the Jewish people, the entire Bible except for possibly the Books of Luke and Acts would not have been written and collected. The whole Bible was written by Jews. No Jews, no Bible. Jesus' earthly parents, Mary and Joseph, were Jews. So, no Jews, no Messiah, and no Savior. Our salvation comes from the Jews.

As we see the uniqueness of Israel and respect it, God puts fresh anointing on us, the Church, we who have been designated as the other unique people. Before God gave Israel the Law and the commandments, He said to Moses, *"You shall be to Me a kingdom of priests and a holy nation"* (Exod. 19:6). This applies to us as well. The God of Israel is your Father, and He has adopted you into His priestly family (see Rom. 9:4-5). God has singled us out. The Bible says that we are *"a chosen generation, a royal priesthood, a holy nation, His own special people"* (1 Pet. 2:9). You are part of a prophetic, apostolic company.

The blessings of Abraham come to us through Jesus Christ. The blessings of Abraham are powerful, for example: *"Whatever you touch will prosper, and you'll be head and not the tail"* (see Deut. 28:9-13). The New Testament tells us that Christ has redeemed us from the curse so that "the blessing of Abraham might come upon the Gentiles in Christ Jesus, that we might receive the promise of the Spirit through faith" (see Gal. 3:14). The ultimate blessing is the indwelling of the Holy Spirit, the promise of the Father.

SHEKINAH

The glory, the manifest, supernatural presence of God, was revealed to the children of Israel, and they called it the "shekinah." It was the Presence of the Holy Spirit. As they walked in obedience, the shekinah stayed with them. In the same way, the Holy Spirit wants to cover you and be with you day and night as you love Him and love the things that He loves.

The shekinah supersedes the politics between Jews and Gentiles. The shekinah reveals our place in the grand scheme of the redemption of the world. God's promises and judgments are in all the earth (see Ps. 105:7).

> *He is the Lord our God; His judgments are in all the earth. Remember His covenant forever, the word which He commanded, for a thousand generations, the covenant which He made with Abraham, and His oath to Isaac, and confirmed it to Jacob for a statute, to Israel for an everlasting covenant, saying, "To you I will give the land of Canaan as the allotment of your inheritance"* (1 Chronicles 16:14-18).

When God makes a promise, He will keep it. His reputation is at stake because of the glory of His name (see Ezek. 36:21). God promised Israel in Ezekiel 36:24-25: *"I will take you from among the nations, gather you out of all countries, and bring you into your own land. Then I will sprinkle clean water on you, and you shall be clean,"* which refers to the Word and the Holy Spirit. And, *"I will put My Spirit within you and cause you to walk in My statutes, and you will keep My judgments and do them. Then you shall dwell in the land that I gave to your fathers; you shall be My people, and I will be your God"* (Ezek. 36:27-28).

THE POWER OF THE CROSS

That's His promise. He's going to bring this people back to give them rebirth and baptism in the Holy Spirit. As the Church observes and applauds this, *"He will set up a banner for the nations, and will assemble the outcasts of Israel, and gather together the dispersed of Judah from the four corners of the earth"* (Isa. 11:12).

In our lifetime, God is up to something awesome, and we've got to listen. The time is coming soon when the children of Israel are going to look at Him whom they have pierced, and He's going to reveal Himself. The return of the Messiah strikes fear into the devil's heart like nothing else, because he knows when *He* comes, he will have lost it all, forever.

As we pray for the peace of Jerusalem, God wants the Church to come together as a loving community that will make the Jews jealous (see Rom. 11:11). He wants our godly lives, our spiritual blessings, our corporate lifestyle, and our joy to display His glory to the people He loves. He wants them to come to our light, to our "dawning brightness" (see Isa. 60:2-3), which is to say, to the shekinah.

GLORY IN HER MIDST

We opened this chapter with a verse from Zechariah *"...I will be the glory in her midst"* (Zech. 2:5). That passage goes on to say,

> *"Sing and rejoice, O daughter of Zion! For behold, I am coming and I will dwell in your midst," says the Lord. "Many nations shall be joined to the Lord in that day, and they shall become My people. And I will dwell in your midst. Then you will know that the Lord of hosts has sent Me to you. And the Lord will take possession of Judah as His inheritance in the Holy Land, and will again choose Jerusalem"* (Zechariah 2:10-12).

A struggle for the spiritual throne of Jerusalem is going on. Jerusalem is the center of our spiritual Kingdom. God called the earthly city of Jerusalem the "pupil of His eye," and declared that whoever touches Jerusalem is poking Him in the eye, incurring His retaliation. In the end, the council of nations is futile:

> *Why do the nations rage, and the people plot a vain thing? The kings of the earth set themselves, and the rulers take counsel together, against the Lord and against His Anointed, saying, "Let us break Their bonds in pieces and cast away Their cords from us." He who sits in the heavens shall laugh; the Lord shall hold them in derision. Then He shall speak to them in His wrath, and distress them in His deep displeasure: "Yet I have set My King on My holy hill of Zion"* (Psalm 2:1-6).

Passages such as this one clearly portray spiritual warfare overlaid with political and earthly conflict. We have an adversary. But we have weapons that are spiritual, mighty to pull down the strongholds thrones, dominions, and kingships set up by the devil on the earth.

> *For though we walk in the flesh, we do not war according to the flesh. For the weapons of our warfare are not carnal but mighty in God for pulling down strongholds, casting down arguments and every high thing that exalts itself against the knowledge of God, bringing every thought into captivity to the obedience of Christ* (2 Corinthians 10:3-5).

Satan, the master of deception, is pouring out the opposing spirit and capturing as many hearts and minds as he can. The final battle is building to a climax, and we have a part to play. Forget about being politically correct. Decide to be scripturally correct. Because of our relationship with the Lord, when His eye gets poked, we feel the pain. As Jesus' Bride, we react when we see the vicious antichrist spirit at work in the world. We know full well that "peace talks" will never work when people are trying to make peace with the antichrist spirit.

Every believer has been called to the side of the Lord in this great spiritual struggle. We are watchmen over Jerusalem and for God's people, Israel. The Church has a vested interest in this epic struggle because we have been grafted into that tree. The Jews have not been grafted into us; we have been grafted into them (see Rom. 11).

We cannot afford to be asleep on these issues. We each have a responsibility as a priest of God, a spiritual ambassador with power, to take a stand and hold it. It is important to stand with Jesus in this battle. He is not confused, and we do not need to be confused, either.

Let's rally daily to the ramparts in prayer, ready for action. Let's pray for the peace of Jerusalem—and for wisdom and a biblical mind-set for the leaders of our nations.

PRAYER FOR JERUSALEM

We pray, O Lord, for the peace of Jerusalem. As your priests and kings, O Lord, as your ambassadors on the earth, in the name of Your holy Son, Jesus, we stretch out the rod of authority over the city Jerusalem and over your people, Israel. May Jehovah Shalom, the Prince of Peace Himself, stand in her midst and give her divine peace. Father, we pray for the hearts of her leaders, that they may have wisdom, discernment, courage, and clarity in this hour. Let the anointing of Isaiah 61 be on the leaders of Your people, O Lord.

As the world looks at Israel and also at the nations who oppose them, we pray, "Your will be done on earth as it is in heaven." The Kingdom belongs to You, Lord. The power belongs to You. Also all wealth, glory, honor, blessing, strength, and dominion.

Father, we pray that all those who would oppose Your purposes and who would harm the people of Israel would be confused today. Make their evil come back on their heads if they will not repent.

Holy Spirit, Comforter, we say, "Come onto Jerusalem like a wedding veil." Come over her gates and portals. Come over her streets and her businesses. Come over her homes and her neighborhoods. Come over her men and women and her children, O God. Come into the hearts of every family that has lost loved ones in the conflict, especially in the past fifty years. Take notice of all the blood that has been shed in the streets of Jerusalem as the nations attempt to divide her and set up their thrones where Your throne is. Come as Comforter and come as the great Defender, we pray.

Hear our prayers, O Lord. Send your glory. In the mighty name of *Yeshua Hamashiach*, the Anointed One, Amen.

ENDNOTES

1. From *The Dream of the Rood,* lines 147-156. Translation copyright © 1982, Jonathan A. Glenn. Used by permission.

2. From *HaTekufa HaGedola*, Rabbi Menachem Kasher, chapter "Sichu B'chol Niflaotav," page 452, 5761 edition, as posted on *Arutz Sheva* (Israel National News) at http://www.israelnationalnews.com/News/News.aspx/122435 in "Miracles in the Six-Day War: Eyewitness Accounts: The Conquest of Shechem."

3. At the time, our television program, *The Watch,* was broadcast twelve times a week across the Arab countries in Arabic translation on Spirit Channel TV.

CHAPTER 10

THE COMING GLORY

Now I command you, loved man of mine,
that you this seeing tell unto men;
discover with words that it is glory's beam
which Almighty God suffered upon
for all mankind's manifold sins
and for the ancient ill-deeds of Adam.
Death he tasted there, yet God rose again
by his great might, a help unto men. [1]

† † † † † † † † † † † † † †

"These cursed Galileans! Infidels! Heretics!" The small dark figure bent over his donkey hurrying along the road was set on a mission that, from his very posture, would frighten the common man.

"Stealing our religion and making a mockery of the inheritance bought with the blood of so many Hebrews," he spat. "It's *their* blood that shall be spilled down to the very last drop of the very last of them before I'm through! God as my witness! Eye for an eye."[2] He raised both hands to Heaven in confident assurance of blessing.

The crooked man with a crooked heart was sure he was straight as an arrow. Striking like lightening. Death in his wake. Stamping out corruption from his pure religion. But his intent was as crooked as his nose, which aside from any family heritage, had been broken once in fisticuffs he had started over the interpretation of a saying from the prophets.

The crooked man had scales over his glaring eyes. And he thought he could see straight.

He watched the road in front of him and thought of the Nazarene. His skin prickled under his pharisaic cloak. Was it the heat or the thought of the Galilean—he could not tell.

The zealot cursed, "He deserved twice the penalty He got!"

The moment the words were out of his mouth, scenes from the last stoning, one of the Nazarene's heretics, a young man, flashed before him. There was something about the one called Stephen—his countenance, his peace, his forgiveness—that had made the crooked man unable to pick up a single stone that day. That had made him...ashamed.

"At least I held the garments of the others while they finished their righteous work!" he consoled himself, refocusing. He knew his Scriptures backward and forward, in two, no three languages. He could recite the exact perspectives of each of the sages' commentaries on the same. He kept a mental list of every regulation down to the last jot. Don't touch! Don't taste! Don't look! Prayer before his feet hit the floor every morning. Tithe down to the half of half a cent on his wages—and tent making kept food in his belly.

He was clean. A Hebrew of Hebrews. Abraham had no better son than he! This was the river of self-approving thoughts swirling about in his balding head. He pulled his tallit forward to prevent the glare of noonday. He was headed north to Damascus on business. His business was stamping out the Nazarene's followers, erasing the very memory of the Man and His disciples, and erasing the taint from Hebrew history.

"I was born out of time! Else it had been me that found Him! Me that turned Him over! Would to Jehovah I could have witnessed His death first hand!"

All this stood him in good stead with those who really mattered. The chief priests themselves had entrusted him with this mission. He hugged the pouch containing their orders, the seal of the Temple firmly stamped in wax.

"Furrow out these Christians giving us trouble in the North! Carry out the full extent of the law as is required in punishing heretics!"

"You shall have no other gods before Me!" he recited worthily. His eyes darted side to side at the company with him. This time he had men under him. A self-satisfied smile came over his lips. He was moving up in the world.

Righteous man among righteous men, he thought smugly. *Thank God, He did not make me a woman!*

His heated heart took courage. He beat furiously upon his burro's rump with the goad, imagining it a rod of correction on the backs of those who followed the Way. As the city rose into view, he dug his heels into the burro's sides.

"Move! Blast you! The sun will be gone entirely before we get into the city! I will have lost a half day that could have been better spent in the cause of the Holy!"

Then it happened.

Lightning—but brighter.

An arrow—a thousand of them, but sharper.

A flash that hid the sun in brightness.

The burro bucked, guffawed, and darted. But it wasn't that which knocked the crooked man to the road, his face in the dust, scrabbling for his purse and his commission. It was the Light.

"Saul!"

He came up to his knees, choking out dirt, groping in darkness. He heard only the soft thudding of sandal soles as his fellows ran away.

"Saul!"

Who knew him here? Who called his name in Aramaic?

"Is it so hard for you to kick against the pricks?"

He struggled but could not get onto his feet. Rubbing the film from his eyes, still he could not see a thing.

"Why are you pursuing Me like a madman?" the Light asked.

He felt as though he was being bathed in fire. He wondered that he didn't smell of smoke. Surely, the little hair on his head had been singed off entirely! He felt for his prayer covering as uncontrolled trembling took him over.

"Lord?—who—who are You?"

"Jesus. Whom you are constantly putting to death. Stand on your feet!"

A cold sweat broke off his neck and poured down Saul's bent back when the Voice spoke again.

"From now on, you work for Me!"

Saul's companions crept back.

"Jonas! Theos! Help me!" Saul swung around in blindness. "Take my hands and guide me. What did you see?"

"Only a flash of light," Theos whispered.

"Knocked us on our backs," Jonas added hoarsely. "What now? Why are we hearing the language of the Galilean?"

"Take me into the city," Saul answered. "To a street called Straight. There we will find our way."

✝ ✝ ✝ ✝ ✝ ✝ ✝ ✝ ✝ ✝ ✝ ✝

God invests the glory of His Son through the Spirit in you and me. The glory is the Presence of the Lord intermingled with the ongoing effective power of Calvary. The cross is daily provision in a supernatural way for our natural life, and we will be caught up in His glory in the resurrection, too. The glory is directly connected to the Holy Spirit. His presence comes and remains on the blood of Jesus. As we become familiar with what the blood is doing for us, the glory will surround us. As long as you have life in your mortal body, the blood will never lose its power, and you need that power. Remember that where the glory is, the blood of the cross is working. Get to know the blood and you will get to know His glory. If you follow the glory, He will lead you to the cross.

Jesus' prayers are filled with glory. The cross is the key to glory:

> *Glorify Your Son, that Your Son also may glorify You....I have glorified You on the earth. I have finished the work which You have given Me to do. And now, O Father, glorify Me together with Yourself, with the glory which I had with You before the world was....And the glory which You gave Me I have given them, that they may be one just as We are one* (John 17:1,4-5,22).

The new creation exceeds the hope and expectation of the first one, just as the Last Adam exceeds the first Adam. In the deep sleep of Calvary, a Bride, the substance of a new race, was drawn from His wounded side. We were raised up by the glory of the Father in Christ's resurrection. The glory of the Father has a name. He is the Holy Spirit. On the cross Christ offered Himself through the Spirit. There God's blood and God's glory mingled to create our future. Sinless flesh and Holy Spirit were united in an explosion of energetic eternal power when Christ died. We were vindicated and made glorious in Him.

JOY UNSPEAKABLE AND FULL OF GLORY

God's glory often appears in the most humble and surprising ways. His glory is never given casually. Our response to God's glory is uproarious joy!

> *Though you have not seen Him, you love Him. Though you do not now see Him, you believe in Him and rejoice*

with joy that is inexpressible and filled with glory
(1 Peter 1:8 ESV).

Derek Prince, our spiritual mentor with whom we served for many years, was the only child of an officer in the British army. Derek was raised in the strictest of environments, sent to boarding schools, and educated at Cambridge. The Christians he knew considered themselves "miserable sinners," which was unappealing to him. While serving with the British army in World War II, he began reading the Bible as a book of philosophy, his field of study at college, and got saved. As the Author of the Book came and looked over his shoulder, Derek was baptized in the Holy Spirit. On the night he was filled with the Spirit, he rolled out of his army cot, hands and feet in the air, laughing uncontrollably.

While we were serving Derek many years later, we got word that a fresh move of God was occurring in the church of some friends who were hosting a South African named Rodney Howard-Browne. To check it out, we took our entire family and went to see for ourselves. On the second night, the preacher turned and made eye contact with our family. In an instant, I (Bonnie) found myself rolling around beneath the pew, laughing uncontrollably. That had never happened to me before! It just goes to show that even a taste of the refreshing Presence will surprise you in a sudden downpour. I was in revival. I was wallowing in "joy unspeakable and full of glory" (see 1 Peter 1:8).

Paul the apostle was an ardent emissary of joy. In every letter he exudes the jubilant spirit of an overcomer. Even when physical bonds held him as a prisoner, Paul was in revival: *"Rejoice in the Lord always. Again I will say, rejoice"* (Phil. 4:4). He also wrote: *"Our hearts ache, but we always have joy. We are poor, but we give spiritual riches to others. We own nothing, and yet we have everything"* (2 Cor. 6:10 NLT). And, *"For the kingdom of God is not eating and drinking, but righteousness and peace and joy in the Holy Spirit"* (Rom. 14:17).

The Gospel anthem goes on. The song never ends. From one generation to the next a new verse, another chorus are added by those who answer Christ's call. The Acts of the Apostles contains the never-ending story. In the last few verses of the last chapter of Acts, Paul is in Rome. Under house arrest then released for a time and arrested again, Paul never bound the Word or the Spirit. He was always a free man in Christ. The last lines recorded from his life are not of his martyrdom, but of his freedom in the power of the Gospel.

> *Then Paul dwelt two whole years in his own rented house, and received all who came to him, preaching the kingdom of God and teaching the things which concern the Lord Jesus Christ with all confidence, no one forbidding him* (Acts 28:30-31).

Every generation has a next chapter to write in the unfolding glory story. We are called through the preaching of the Gospel in order that we obtain glory (see 2 Thess. 2:14). Glory is eternal (see 1 Tim. 1:17). Every Christian is a living letter, a message proclaimed to all who know them. This story will come to a climax when its Author and Hero appear from Heaven. There is no end to the glory story.

RECOVERY TIME

Awhile back, the Lord spoke to me (Bonnie) and said, "If you obey My voice, you will recover what you have lost." I had misplaced some cash a couple of months earlier. I was like the woman in the parable who lost a coin and swept her house searching for it. I looked high and low but couldn't find my treasure. I worried about what had happened to it.

One night on the way home from a meeting, the Lord showed me a vision. I saw myself speaking to a workman who had done some repairs on our home. I heard specific words for this man and saw that I was to sow something into his life. When I got home, I went to get that treasure, and next to it, I found the treasure that had been missing! The next morning I waited for the workman to come collect his tools. I knew the Lord was going to meet him. But the man didn't come. I had another appointment, and so had to leave. As I went out the door, he came walking up our driveway. I gave him the word of the Lord and the presence of God settled over us. The man's heart melted in the liquid love of the Father, and he began to physically shake as the Holy Spirit coursed through his body. He had grown up as a Christian, but had gone away from the Lord and his guilt was holding him captive. As we prayed, he came home to his heavenly Father's embrace. I sowed a gift into his "recovery." The Father was searching for His treasure. He sent me looking for His missing son and I recovered the treasure I had lost too!

We are in a season of spiritual recovery. It's a time of return. The manifest glory of the Lord's presence has been missing from Church expression for many years. It's recovery time now. *"Awake, O sleeper, and arise from the dead, and Christ will shine on you"* (Eph. 5:14 ESV).

The "last days" described in the Bible are all around us. There's a whole lot of shaking going on. Times of shaking always precede times of glory. If you want to display a diamond, you put it on the darkest background you can find, and then shine a bright light on it. The light of the glory of God is rising on His Bride. Suddenly, in times of difficulty and increasing darkness in many places, the doors of opportunity are opening for Christians everywhere. Believers are finding the opportunity to realize their unfulfilled dreams. This is a set-up from Heaven. It's your time to rise and shine!

Changing Values

"God, use me!" Does that sound familiar? The difficult circumstances of our life are sometimes the very answer to our prayers. There's a story in 2 Kings chapter 5 that shows us how to recognize the glory of God.

Naaman was a mighty man. As commander of Syria's army, he was highly esteemed by his king. He was responsible for Syria's supremacy over Israel. But Naaman was a leper. All his human influence and strength was useless at the point of his need. A daughter from Israel, abducted during one of Naaman's raids, was a slave in his household. A slave with the heart of a servant became the vessel of glory who carried the word of healing for her master.

The slave-girl said, *"Would that my lord were with the prophet who is in Samaria! He would cure him of his leprosy"* (2 Kings 5:2 ESV). She made herself a messenger of God's blessing for the very person who had enslaved her.

Naaman went to his king and told him what the girl from Israel had said. "By all means, go," the king of Aram replied. "I will send a letter to the king of Israel" (see 2 Kings 5:5). So Naaman took 750 pounds of silver and 75 pounds of gold, plus several valuable festival garments. By today's standard that's 2.5 million dollars in silver and gold alone! It required an entourage of servants, ranks of soldiers, and a train of donkeys to carry all of this treasure.

The king of Israel received Naaman. And when the king read the letter, he said, *"Am I God, to kill and to make alive, that this man sends word to me to cure a man of his leprosy? Only consider, and see how he is seeking a quarrel with me"* (2 Kings 5:7 ESV). Elisha heard about it and sent a message: "Send the man to me."

So Naaman and his entourage arrived at the prophet's house with all that loot. Naaman expected to be received in a manner important people were accustomed to, but Elisha didn't even come out to meet him. Instead he sent his servant to tell Naaman, *"Go and wash in the Jordan seven times, and your flesh shall be restored, and you shall be clean"* (2 Kings 5:10 ESV).

What would you have done if you were in Elisha's shoes? Our culture is obsessed with a "super-star" mentality, both inside and outside the Church. But God is changing our value system. He was about to change Naaman's value system too. Elisha's reception offended the great man:

> *'Behold, I thought that he would surely come out to me and stand and call upon the name of the Lord his God, and wave his hand over the place and cure the leper. Are not Abana and Pharpar, the rivers of Damascus, better than all the waters of Israel? Could I not wash in them and be clean?' So he turned and went away in a rage* (2 Kings 5:11-12 ESV).

Naaman would have to humble himself to get the revelation. The commander stood on the threshold of receiving a miracle. He was willing to offer a great treasure for it, but his pride almost kept him from his healing. Once again, it was a servant who suggested, *"My father, it is a great word the prophet has spoken to you; will you not do it? Has he actually said to you, 'Wash, and be clean'?"* (2 Kings 5:13 ESV).

The glory of the cross is magnified throughout Naaman's story. In Christ, the way up is down! As the ultimate Servant, Jesus utterly humbled Himself, and the Father gave Him the name above name. God has chosen the low road as the pathway to glory. His *servants* become connectors to the glory and to miracles for themselves and others. The Holy Spirit is God Almighty, and He is a Servant, too.

Naaman went down the mountain. He went down to the river. He laid down his proud garments and stood naked and lowly on the bank of the muddy Jordan. His soldiers and servants were surely appalled when they saw their master's condition. They must have watched in amazement as Naaman obeyed the word of servants.

The Jordan is a symbol of death. Its water is a type of the blood that flowed down from Calvary's fountain. The proud have an aversion to it. The cross is the very last place a proud person would go for help. But that humble flow cleanses the vilest stains. Jesus spoke seven words as He shed His blood. Naaman dipped seven times in the Jordan. The cross provides our complete salvation. Naaman was completely healed inside and out. Be they great or lowly, weak or strong, every person that washes in the blood of the cross will possess the glories of Heaven.

You may be on dip number three. You may be on dip number four, five, or six. You may feel like Naaman did on the mountain, a little angry and ready to go away. You may have already paid a great price. God does not always show up in the time or way that we expect. Sometimes He offends our minds to get to our hearts. He responds to simple acts of humility and obedience. Childlike faith is the gateway to great miracles. Remember that Jesus was baptized in the muddy Jordan, and the glory came down. He came down to rest on the Lamb.

Naaman offered the prophet gold and silver in payment for his healing. Elisha refused. He was living according to God's value system. Naaman still had something to learn. You cannot purchase or earn or repay this salvation. You can only humble yourself and embrace it.

Standing in the glory on the mountain, Naaman got a revelation. He wanted a token of the place where he was healed: "Please let me, your servant, be given as much earth as a pair of mules can carry" (see 2 Kings 5:17). A few pounds of dirt from the place of the glory meant more to him than the treasure of kings. God's glory can be shared, received, recognized, and given away. It was purchased with blood—the blood of the Lamb, the most precious treasure.

Naaman took his two donkeys of dirt back to his pagan homeland. He built an altar of worship to the God of Israel. Imagine how that impacted Syria's strategy of war. The commander of Syria's armies became a *prayer* warrior for his former enemies when he was touched by God's glory!

Naaman's healing was more than skin deep. He walked out of the river as changed on the inside as he was on the outside. When he went back to the mountain, Elisha came out to meet him. Naaman's seven-fold washing is a type of coming to Calvary. It's the way to a face-to-face meeting with God.

A WORD FROM GLORY

Years ago, I (Mahesh) was in a hospital waiting room. With me were three people who had brought me to pray for a young girl who was dying of cancer. I said, "Well, while we wait, let's just invite the Holy Spirit to come." There were eighteen other people, all strangers to us, in the waiting room. I simply said within the hearing of my three companions, "Welcome, Holy Spirit." The next thing I knew, everyone in the waiting room—all eighteen plus my three—were on the floor. If a glimpse of God's glory is enough to do that, and we are carriers of His glory, we should expect the unexpected.

"For the earth will be filled with the knowledge of the glory of the Lord as the waters cover the sea" (Hab. 2:14). God's glory is more tangible than you might think. His glory shines like the sun. When Moses said, *"Show me Your glory,"* he was saying, "I want *more* of You, God." Moses had been on the mountain in the presence of the Lord for over a month, and that was not enough. Once you experience God's presence, you will never get enough. You can welcome Him now. His glory will fill your heart and bring transformation where you are. Every time He gives you a taste, get hungry for more.

Glory and grace will increase as long as your heart desires. God wants to take us from glory to glory!

When our baby Aaron was born at just 25 weeks, he weighed barely one pound. As Aaron lay dying in a Florida hospital, I (Mahesh) was ministering in Africa. I had said goodbye to my son, thinking it would be the last time I would see him in this world. Across the ocean in Kinshasa, Zaire, the Lord stepped in to show me His glory. One hot afternoon I was ministering to a crowd of Africans who were desperate for miracles. The service had ended and I had stepped away from the microphone when suddenly everything changed. It seemed I was surrounded by music. A vibration from Heaven swirled around me, and I heard the Lord say, "There is a man here whose son died this morning. Call him up because today I am going to do a great thing." When I gave the word, a man came running out of the crowd. "It's me! It's me! My son died this morning!" Mulamba Manikai's six-year-old son had died of cerebral malaria. As I prayed, the Holy Spirit came down and His glory rolled out across the city to the morgue where Katshinyi's body lay. The dead boy suddenly sneezed twice and sat up. And that's not the end of the story. The glory kept on rolling back across the ocean. The same Holy Spirit that raised the African boy touched our son. Today Aaron is completely whole. Miracles begin with a word from the glory.

GREATER GLORY

Every time you respond to the Lord, glory accrues in your divine bank account. Cultivate God's presence. Eventually blessings will spill over. The presence of God's glory in you will start to affect other people around you. As you learn to host His presence, you will find yourself walking in miracles plus. It was a miracle when Katshinyi was resurrected from the dead, and the plus was Aaron's healing.

If you are going for greater glory, here are some things you can do:

Earnestly desire His presence and His glory will come more and more: *"And you will seek Me and find Me, when you search for Me with all your heart"* (Jer. 29:13).

Obey His written word: *"If you love Me, keep My commandments..."* (John 14:15). His word is full of power. It will wash you, renew and transform you. Your relationship with God develops as you commune with Him. His word is key to staying in the glory.

Get connected in a Spirit-filled, local church body. To get in harmony with Heaven you have to get into harmony with fellow believers. There's no harmony if you are singing solo.

Honor spiritual authority: *"Obey those who rule over you, and be submissive, for they watch out for your souls, as those who must give account"* (Heb. 13:17a). The glory is a culture of honor. God has created us to be interdependent with Him and with one another.

Be filled and be regularly re-filled with the Holy Spirit. Praying in tongues is one of the ways to increase your faith, *"building yourselves up in your most holy faith and praying in the Holy Spirit"* (Jude 1:20). Your prayer language is the mother tongue of Heaven. Use it to connect with the glory.

Learn to be led by the Spirit: *"For as many as are led by the Spirit of God, these are sons of God"* (Rom. 8:14). The Holy Spirit searches the deep things of God. He teaches us, He guides us, He helps us, He intercedes for us, and He transforms us into the likeness of His glory.

Look to the cross: *"But God forbid that I should glory, save in the cross of our Lord Jesus Christ, by whom the world is crucified unto me, and I unto the world"* (Gal. 6:14 KJV). Always be aware that the blood is working on your behalf. The cross is your pathway to power and the gateway to living in harmony with Heaven.

Learn to be thankful for everything: *"in everything give thanks; for this is the will of God in Christ Jesus for you"* (1 Thess. 5:18). Glory is vocalized in praise (see 1 Chron. 16:28). Glory is wealth, majesty, dignity, and splendor. Engage in praising the Lord of glory, and your awareness of His presence will increase.

Keep a perpetual melody going in your heart. Sing in the Spirit, and make God's throne in your spirit *BIG*. He inhabits the praise of His people. Worship is the passport to the Land of No Limits.

> *...be filled with the Spirit, speaking to one another in psalms and hymns and spiritual songs, singing and making melody in your heart to the Lord, giving thanks always for all things to God the Father in the name of our Lord Jesus Christ* (Ephesians 5:18-20).

Make a decision to trust in the Lord at all times and in all situations. He will bring things into wholeness and peace. Fear can break your connection with the vibration of Heaven. Make Jesus your security today. *"Do good and do not fear anything that is frightening"* (1 Pet. 3:6 ESV).

MAKING MUSIC WITH HEAVEN

One encounter with God is just the beginning. We want to keep on cooperating with the waves of His glory:

> *Nothing between us and God, our faces shining with the brightness of His face. And so we are transfigured much like the Messiah, our lives gradually becoming brighter and more beautiful as God enters our lives and we become like Him* (2 Corinthians 3:18 TM).

The more we are in tune with the Holy Spirit, the more our hearts will sing. We are God's instruments. Each of us has been invited into the symphony God is conducting. The whole world is beginning to pick up the melody—it is the sound of His appearing. You can sing along. Don't wait for your circumstances to change. Create the change around you by picking up the glory vibration coming from the cross. There's joy in the glory. There's healing in the glory. There are answers for each situation. It's Jesus. He is with us in the cloud of His Spirit and He is singing salvation's song.

When I (Mahesh) was recovering from back surgery, I needed to use a wheelchair in airports. I had a friend with me to help with my baggage, but an airline employee had to bring me a wheelchair and transport me. We were in the Portland airport, and a young woman was pushing the wheelchair. Suddenly, she stopped, and she was crying.

"What's wrong?" I said.

She went a little farther, and then she stopped and started crying again. She bent down and said, "Who are you? I have never felt the presence of God like this in my life!"

I answered, "Oh, I give lectures." I didn't want to tell her what I lecture about until I could figure out what was happening.

We went a little farther, with my friend walking alongside. Again the young woman stopped walking and started crying, saying, "I really have never felt God like this in my life. Who are you?"

This time, I said, "Well, we are servants of God."

By the time we arrived at the baggage claim, she got down on her knees before hundreds of people and received Jesus. We had hardly uttered a word. God's glory made it happen. All we did was stay near Him and let that girl get near Him, too. We are the messengers of His cross and the carriers of His glory.

The Holy Spirit is all around you. You can become an agent of transformation as you cultivate His presence. The melody of the

Spirit should become your primary life-song. You will be singing along with Heaven. The angels will be attending you and darkness will fly away!

THE BLOOD MAKES THE WAY

The blood of Christ is not a 2,000-year-old paint job dried on an ancient wooden instrument of execution. The blood is ever fresh, ever living, ever present, ever working, now and later. The glory and the cross are companions. The cross makes the way for the glory. The blood speaks, calling us home.

Our relationship with the glory through the blood welcomes transformation. As we have received His death we have received His life. Where the blood is the Holy Spirit is. He makes full provision in light and dark, heat and cold. In every situation Christ is present and working in you by His Spirit. The blood makes way for the cloud. Whether it is light or dark around us, we have Him as a covering. The blood changes everything. How can anyone resist this miracle?

The foretastes of God's glory we are experiencing—the awareness of His Presence, His miracles and answered prayers—are all the Holy Spirit with us in the presence of the eternal blood of Christ. The Spirit comes alongside to wrap us in glory and prepare the Bride for her Husband. Where the Spirit is there is glory. In the resurrection, our body will be redeemed, changed into a glorious spiritual body fit for eternal habitation just like Christ's glorious one. The Spirit who raised Christ and who works in us will raise us up with Him in glory. The Spirit of adoption is breathing His eternal breath of life into our mortal being. He will bring us face to face with our Father.

At the judgment, we will have an Advocate, the testimony of Christ and the Holy Spirit before the Father against every sin and all accusers. We will be acquitted as righteous and released from an eternal death sentence. Our names will have been inscribed in the Lamb's book of life and not blotted out. O, the humility of God! O, the love! O, the mercy! O, the power! O, the wonder! What glory indeed has been shared with those who love Him!

Some people live their whole lives with a mental assent toward religion, but you can have the reality. You can know Him. You can get to know His blood. You can be intimately acquainted with His Spirit. The Servant Spirit has been sent by the Father as Ambassador of the Son to be in us and with us. This is the glory every believer receives as inheritance. We have been made His sons. He dwells within us personally and creates a spiritual tabernacle that will be changed into the glorious eternal Temple because of the Cross.

As long as we have life in a body of flesh, the cross makes way for the glory. We share now in the glory to come. The cloud that covered Israel, resting on the blood that was sprinkled on the ark covers you now:

> *In the daytime also He led them with the cloud, and all the night with a light of fire. He split the rocks in the wilderness, and gave them drink in abundance like the depths. He also brought streams out of the rock, and caused waters to run down like rivers* (Psalm 78:14-16).

As we acknowledge Him, we are becoming aware of His Presence. We are awakening to the reality that we are standing near the cross, in fact, beneath its very shadow. It towers above us as a glorious banner of victory, the pedestal of the Ardent Champion, the high tower to which we run for refuge and deliverance. It shouts as it stands over us, the ensign of our peace, the crest of our family name, the beacon of our heritage. There atop Golgotha's hill, is that blessed tree where suffering is transformed into eternal glory! That is the place of our sanctification, the place of our unification. The Glorious One draws us to Himself there. He is attracted to all who come to Him there. On that mountain of mountains, the chief hill, the cloud of God's Spirit responds to the ruddy flow of our Savior's wounds. There comes the Comforter, wrapping us in light. There we find our true selves. There we are set free.

> *Now it shall come to pass in the latter days that the mountain of the Lord's house shall be established on the top of the mountains, and shall be exalted above the hills; and all nations shall flow to it. Many people shall come and say, "Come, and let us go up to the mountain of the Lord, to the house of the God of Jacob; He will teach us His ways, and we shall walk in His paths." For out of Zion shall go forth the law, and the word of the Lord from Jerusalem* (Isaiah 2:2-3).

YES! YES! YES!

I (Mahesh) was recently at the Airport Church famous for the "Toronto Revival." While ministering in the evening service, I got in tune with the melody of the glory. I started sharing with about a thousand people. We began to pick up a vibration from glory coming through the Word:

> *Have you ever come on anything quite like this extravagant generosity of God, this deep, deep wisdom? It's way over our heads. We'll never figure it out....Everything comes from Him; Everything happens through Him; Everything ends up in Him. Always glory! Always praise! Yes. Yes. Yes* (Romans 11:33-36 TM).

It ended in a glory chant. As I declared, "Always Glory, Always Praise, Yes. Yes. Yes." The congregation joyfully and in unison took up the chant:

"Always Glory! Always Praise! Yes. Yes. Yes.

Always Glory! Always Praise! Yes. Yes. Yes"

I sensed that triumphant atmosphere was touching someone's loved one, bringing that person out of a coma.

I said, "Where is the person whose loved one is in a coma?"

A young lady named Amy from Traverse City came up.

I asked, "Who are you standing in for?"

With tear-filled eyes and a trembling voice she said, "My friend Joseph. He was in a car accident on Monday, and now he is in a coma."

"How old is he?"

"Seventeen."

I said, "The Lord is here to touch Joseph tonight," and I prayed that the same glory bubble that was in our meeting would go and touch Joseph in the hospital.

The next day Amy told us, "You prayed for me at 10:21 last night. At 10:32, eleven minutes later, I got a text message. It was from Joseph. He told me he just woke up!"

God's glory has no limits in time or space. The same glory that touched Joseph is the glory flowing through you and me now.

From the earth to the cross, from the cross to the grave, from the grave to the mountain, and up to the throne, the King of glory has taken His place. There He stands—the Lamb who was slain—surrounded by angels and elders and fire. A rainbow is surrounding His throne as the four living creatures cry, "Holy!" In thunder and lightning and voices, His blood is speaking for you.

When we finally see Him face to face, our adventure will just be beginning. Until then, we keep on believing, keep on receiving, and keep our hearts fixed on true treasure. When your heart is steadfast toward the King of Calvary, you suddenly find that you are a central figure in His never-ending glory story. The dreamer has awakened. Day by day the vision that leads him is the blood-drenched, jewel-bedecked gallows. And so we revert to the Rood:

> *For me now life's hope:*
> *that I may seek that victory-beam...*
> *my hope of protection*
> *reverts to the rood...*
> *and I for myself expect*
> *each of my days the time when the Lord's rood,*
> *which I here on earth formerly saw,*
> *from this loaned life will fetch me away*
> *and bring me then where is much bliss.*[3]

The cross of Jesus Christ is the epicenter of glory. It stands upright with His victory on display. Ultimately, even death moves in the face of the Lamb. Praise the Lord for His glorious work on Calvary. Praise the Lord for the power of His resurrection. Praise the Lord, for He is exalted among the nations. Praise the Lord, His glory shall cover the earth as the waters cover the sea! With His saints and the angels, a great company of heroes, we are joining in the anthem we can hear:

Always Glory! Always Praise! Yes! Yes!. Yes!

Always Glory! Always Praise! Yes! Yes! Yes!

ENDNOTES

1. From *The Dream of the Rood,* lines 95-102. Translation copyright © 1982, Jonathan A. Glenn. Used by permission.

2. See Exodus 21:24.

3. From *The Dream of the Rood,* lines 126-127, 130-131, 135-139. Translation copyright © 1982, Jonathan A. Glenn. Used by permission.

MAHESH AND BONNIE CHAVDA

CONTACT INFORMATION

Chavda Ministries International
P.O. Box 411008
Charlotte, NC 28241
Phone: 1-800-730-6264
Fax: 704-541-5300
Email: info@chavdaministries.org
Website: chavdaministries.org

DESTINY IMAGE PUBLISHERS, INC.

"Speaking to the Purposes of God for This Generation
and for the Generations to Come."

VISIT OUR NEW SITE HOME AT
WWW.DESTINYIMAGE.COM

FREE SUBSCRIPTION TO DI NEWSLETTER

Receive free unpublished articles by top DI authors, exclusive
discounts, and free downloads from our best and newest books.
Visit www.destinyimage.com to subscribe.

Write to: Destiny Image
              P.O. Box 310
              Shippensburg, PA 17257-0310

Call: 1-800-722-6774

Email: orders@destinyimage.com

For a complete list of our titles or to place an order
online, visit www.destinyimage.com.

FIND US ON FACEBOOK OR FOLLOW US ON TWITTER.

www.facebook.com/destinyimage   facebook
www.twitter.com/destinyimage   twitter